THE
NIGHT
THE
BEAR
ATE
GOOMBAW

Also by Patrick F. McManus

Kid Camping from Aaaaiii! to Zip
A Fine and Pleasant Misery
They Shoot Canoes, Don't They?
Never Sniff a Gift Fish
The Grasshopper Trap
Rubber Legs and White Tail-Hairs

THE
NIGHT
THE
BEAR
ATE
GOOMBAW

Patrick F. McManus

Henry Holt and Company • New York

To Vern Schulze, without whom many
of these stories would never have happened

Published by Henry Holt and Company, Inc.,
115 West 18th Street, New York, New York 10011.
Published in Canada by Fitzhenry & Whiteside Limited,
195 Allstate Parkway, Markham, Ontario L3R 4T8.

Library of Congress Cataloging-in-Publication Data
McManus, Patrick F.
The night the bear ate Goombaw / Patrick F. McManus. —1st ed.
p.   cm.
ISBN 0–8050–1033–5
1. Outdoor recreation—United States—Humor.   I. Title.
PN6162.M349   1989   88–34618
813'.54—dc19   CIP

Henry Holt books are available at special discounts for
bulk purchases for sales promotions, premiums, fund-
raising, or educational use. Special editions or book
excerpts can also be created to specification. For details
contact: Special Sales Director, Henry Holt and Company, Inc.
115 West 18th Street, New York, New York 10011.

FIRST EDITION

Designed by Claire M. Naylon
Printed in the United States of America
3   5   7   9   10   8   6   4

All stories in this book appeared previously as follows: In *Field & Stream*: "Scritch's Creek" (originally titled "Scritch's Crick"). In *Johnson Outboards Boating*: "Gunkholing" (originally titled "I'd Rather Be . . . Gunkholing"). In *Outdoor Life*: "Blips"; "The Night the Bear Ate Goombaw"; "Water Spirits" (originally titled "Spirits"); "Letter to the Boss" (originally titled "Letter to My Boss"); "A Road Less Traveled By"; "The Fried Flies, Please, and Easy on the Garlic" (originally titled "Lord of the Flies"); "How to Get Started in Bass Fishing" (originally titled "The Beginner's Guide to Bass Fishing"); "At Loose Ends" (originally titled "Tying One On"); "Sequences"; "Kid Brothers and Their Practical Application"; "Garage-Sale Hype" (originally titled "Garage-Sale Frenzy"); "Scoring"; "Out of Sync"; "Cupidity, Draw Thy Bow" (originally titled "Love Me, Love My Bass"); "The Tin Horn"; "The Dumbest Antelope"; "Visions of Fish and Game"; "Whitewater Fever"; "Never Cry 'Arp!' "; "Getting It in the Ear"; "As the Worm Squirms"; "Try Not to Annoy Me"; "A Brief History of Boats and Marriage"; "Boating Disorders."

Contents

THE
NIGHT
THE
BEAR
ATE
GOOMBAW

Sequences

I have long been a student of sequences, probably because of my upbringing on a farm and, perhaps the larger influence, my association with my stepfather, Hank. My mother remarried several years after my father died, and Hank came to live with us on our Idaho farm. He was a city person, at one time the manager of a minor-league baseball team who had spent most of his working life in the grocery business. You would expect that someone in the grocery business would know about farming and sequences, but both forever remained a mystery to Hank.

What Hank seemed never able to grasp was that on a farm you simply don't go out and do a piece of work. No, the first thing you do is determine the lengthy sequence of activities necessary even to begin the job. Then you realize that the sequence of preparatory activities is so long you will never get to the intended task. So you go fishing instead. This had been my family's approach to farming for generations, and it worked fine, but Hank could just never get the hang of it.

One day Hank said to me, "Pat, let's take off the day and go fishing up Ruby Crick."

"Sounds good to me," I said. "Let's go."

"Okay. But first we have to fix that hole in the pasture fence. Won't take but twenty minutes."

My shoulders sagged. "Hank," I said. "Either we go fishing or we fix the fence. Which is it?"

"Both," he said. "First we fix the fence, then we go fishing. Now go get the wire stretcher and we'll get started."

I saw that it was hopeless. No matter how often I had tried to explain sequences to Hank, he could never grasp their significance. "The wire stretcher's broken," I said.

"Oh, that's right. Well, we'll just run over to the Haversteads and borrow theirs."

"Yeah, but the Malloys borrowed our post-hole digger."

"We can swing by the Malloys and pick up our post-hole digger on the way back from borrowing the Haversteads' wire stretcher. Then we fix the fence and go fishing. Easy as pie."

"We're out of fence staples, too."

"Is that right? I guess after we borrow the Haversteads' wire stretcher and pick up our post-hole digger from the Malloys, we can zip into town and buy some staples at Jergans Hardware, come back, fix the fence, and go fishing."

"But Hank, you promised Sam Jergans you would haul him in a load of hay bales from the Nelsons' the next time you came to town."

"Danged if that ain't what I promised! I got to take Sam the hay when we go for the staples. Otherwise he'll be mad as hops. We'll have to take the truck, but first we better pick up the spare tire that's over at LaRoy's Shop getting fixed. So here's what we'll do. We'll borrow the post-hole digger from the Haversteads, pick up our wire stretcher from the Malloys, stop by LaRoy's Shop and get the spare, go over to Nelson's and load the hay, haul the hay in to Jergans, buy the staples, come home, fix the fence, and go fishing. How does that sound?"

"You're getting mixed up, Hank. We borrow the wire stretcher from the Haversteads and pick up our post-hole digger from the Malloys."

"Good leapin' gosh a'mighty, this is gettin' complicated. Now where did we start? I better write it down in the proper . . . "

"Sequence," I said. "We started out to go fishing, but first you wanted to fix that stupid hole in the fence."

It was this early training in sequences that made almost any endeavor in life seem impossible to me. That is why I have just gone fishing instead. I have always enjoyed reading about the great successes so many men and women achieve, and once I even thought I would read a book about how to become a success myself.

"I'm going down to the library to check out a book that tells me how I can become a success," I told my wife, Bun.

"That's a good idea," she said. "I only wish you had read it thirty years ago. Since you're going downtown to the library, will you drop off some clothes at the dry cleaners?"

"Sure."

"I have a coupon for twenty-five percent discount on cleaning. Oh, darn! I threw the newspaper out. Will you run over to the Smiths and see if they still have theirs? And I told Bev Smith she could have that old trunk in the attic and you can take it over to her when you go, but you'll have to repair the hinge on the attic door first, because otherwise the door will fall off, so when you're down in the basement getting your tool box, I'd like you to—"

"Forget it," I said. "I'm going fishing."

I never did get to read the book on how to become a success. I doubt if I missed much. Once I did go to a seminar on becoming a success, and the speaker said the most important thing was for one to set goals for oneself. That was when I walked out. Any fool can set goals. I've set more goals than a trapper sets traps. I could set half a dozen goals for myself this very minute, without exerting more than a couple of brain cells in the process. The problem is getting to the goals. Every goal has a sequence swirling beneath it like the vortex of a whirlpool. Take your first step toward that goal and you're instantly sucked into the vortex, swirled downward endlessly farther and farther away from your goal, until you've completely forgotten what the goal was, and your only concern is how to get out of the vortex. It's kind of scary, if you think about it.

I've seen decent, normal persons suddenly come down with ambition and set themselves a goal or two. Then they set off for their goals and you hear a diminishing wail as they're sucked down into the vortex of sequence, and they're never seen again, although sometimes you'll get a postcard from Acapulco. It's much better just to go fishing and forget about success. You'll be happier, take my word for it.

Even fishing can be fraught with sequence, however, and you must be constantly on guard against it. Suppose, for example, Retch Sweeney shows up and asks me to go fishing with him. I say, "Okay," grab rod, reel, and tackle box, and start out the door.

"What test line you got on that reel?" Retch asks.

"Four-pound."

"Not strong enough for bass. Go put eight-pound on. Ten would be better."

"Do you want to fish or get sucked into a sequential vortex?" I snap, continuing on out the door.

"What? You got trouble with your drains again? Yeah, let's get outta here before Bun catches us. Four-pound's good enough."

I have never attempted to explain sequences to Retch, but he has an instinct for avoiding them. Somewhere in the spacious recesses of his mind he senses that if I wait to put on eight-pound line before I go fishing, I will never get to the fishing. Maybe there won't be quite enough line to fill the spool. Then I will have to wind the line off the reel spool and back onto the stock spool. Next I will have to find some line to back up the eight-pound line. After that I will have to go to Gary Soucie's *Hook, Line & Sinker* to study the knot for tying two lines together. But then I'll remember I loaned the book to my next-door neighbor, Al Finley, but if I go ask Finley for it, he will want his lawn mower back before Bun has a chance to mow the lawn with it. Thus I will be forced to mow the lawn myself, then return the lawn mower to Finley, get my book back, study the knot, tie the two lines together, and wind them on the spool. By then it will be too late to go fishing. It's better to take my chances with four-pound-test.

If you are to achieve any happiness in this world or know a moment's peace, you must learn to view any undertaking not as an isolated event in itself but as a starting point from which you work backwards through endless sequences. The happiest man I ever knew was my old mentor in woodscraft, Rancid Crabtree. Rancid understood the necessity of avoiding sequences. "You can't go chasin' life all over tarnation," he was fond of saying. "You got to set back and let it come to you. Stay in one place long enough and most everthang'll come by at least once."

It didn't make any sense to me either. But the point is, Rancid was the happiest man I've ever known. Faced with some monumental task or dismal but necessary chore, he didn't sit around whining or cursing his luck. He just squared his shoulders, set his jaw, and said, "This dang nuisance can take care of itself. Let's go fishin'!"

The man knew sequences.

The Dumbest Antelope

Mr. Clare Conley
Editor-in-Chief
Outdoor Life
New York, N.Y.

Dear Clare:
At this very minute, *Outdoor Life*'s executive
editor, the wily Vin Sparano, is racing hellbent for
vinyl back to New York to give you his version of the
antelope hunt in Wyoming. Don't believe a word he says.
His account of the trip will be nothing but lies, designed
to put all the blame on me. I am rushing this letter off
to you by express mail, so that you will have in hand the
true facts of the matter before Vin arrives. But first,
here is a list of my expenses for the trip:

Airfare.................................... $380.00
Meals $46.15
Rental of four-wheel-drive vehicle $405.26

Fuel	$212.35
Tips	$00.75
Miscellaneous	$24,478.54

Please note my frugality, tipping serving as an excellent example of my effort to hold costs to a minimum. Any questions?

Oh, perhaps I should explain something about Miscellaneous. As you probably know, there is a Wyoming law that all males over age five must wear cowboy hats. My hat cost $150. Since wearing a cowboy hat without cowboy boots looks ridiculous, I picked up a pair of them too—$200. I thought the spurs ($65) would add a nice touch. The leather vest, plaid shirt, and kerchief came to roughly $180—it's a very nice vest. Now for my great bargain, a really nifty pair of chaps for—would you believe?—$140. Normally you can't buy a pair of woolly chaps for anywhere near that price.

That's about it for Miscellaneous, except for a few other odds and ends that slip my mind at the moment. Now let me give you the true facts about the antelope hunt.

To begin with, I flew into Rock Springs, Wyoming, rented a four-wheel-drive vehicle, and drove eight hundred miles to Rawlins. True, the normal driving distance between Rock Springs and Rawlins is less than one hundred miles, but only if you make a right turn instead of a left turn leaving Rock Springs. The left turn takes you to Rawlins by way of Montana, a very scenic route, believe me, and one that definitely should be put on the map.

An elderly rancher, who claimed mine was the first "strange face" he had seen in that part of Wyoming in the last four years, finally got me pointed in the general direction of Rawlins. He said just follow the signs. All the signs, however, had been made by deer and antelope, few of which had been heading for Rawlins. The rancher, by the way, complimented me on my woolly chaps, after he got over his first impression that I was trying to steal two of his sheep, or so he claimed. We both thought that very amusing, he somewhat more than I. He warned me not to wear them into any of the tougher Wyoming saloons, no doubt fearful that one of the cowboys there might try to make off with them for his own use, such is the rarity of woolly chaps nowadays in Wyoming.

I eventually found Rawlins and made my way to the hunting camp some miles north of the town. Right away I saw I was about to fall in with bad company—Vin Sparano, editor and writer; Jim Zumbo, editor and writer; Bill Rooney, editor and writer; Hal Nesbitt, editor and writer; Kathy Etling, writer; and Bob Etling, a normal person. A rougher bunch probably hadn't been assembled in Wyoming since the Hole-in-the-Wall gang broke up. There were characters here who could quick-draw a library card and check out three books faster than the eye could follow. Others could split an infinitive with a single blow and not think twice about it. Sparano was said to smile while firing off rejection slips with both hands.

I got Zumbo aside. "This looks more like a literary convention than a hunting trip," I told him. "I don't want to show these people up, or you either. Sure, I don't mind giving everybody a few hunting tips, but it's embarrassing for them when I fill my tag right away and they're bumbling around day after day, hoping against hope that they might luck out and get a close, standing shot."

"You don't have to worry," Zumbo said. "They'll do fine. Besides, Hal and I have already gotten our antelopes."

"You have? Hal too?"

Harold "Hal" Nesbitt happens to be the administrative director of the Boone & Crockett Club. I was happy to hear he had already got his antelope because that would leave him free to score my antelope before any shrinkage occurred. Typically, my big game trophies shrink as much as 50 percent before they can be measured, thus denying me admission to the Boone & Crockett record book. With Hal right there, this problem was as good as solved.

As you might expect, Zumbo had selected the worst possible camping site in all of Wyoming, a knob of ground surrounded on all sides by wide-open spaces as far as the eye could see. Since the camp had no restroom facilities and the tallest bush was less than a foot high, any calls of nature could be answered only by hiking out toward the horizon until one was concealed by the curvature of the earth. Just going to the bathroom took up half the day.

Shelter consisted of a small camping trailer and a motor home. Sparano and Rooney slept on the bed in the camper and Nesbitt and I slept on the table. I slept with all my clothes on, not only because I didn't know Hal that well but because my sleeping bag is rated at only ten degrees below zero. The first night I scarcely got a wink of sleep. Hal tossed and turned all night, complaining about stabbing pains in his legs. I would have got up and slept on the floor, except I thought the jangling of my spurs might wake the others.

The next day's hunting proved thoroughly disappointing. Everyone but me got an antelope. Vin made a lucky long shot. I say lucky because the antelope in question was so far away as not to be visible to the naked eye. Vin explained—and explained and explained—how he had held 503 feet above the animal and led it by a quarter of a mile, working into his calculations the factors of wind, temperature, humidity, and level of suspended particles in the air. My theory is that Vin fired a shot to test his rifle and an antelope came by several minutes later and accidentally got into the line of fire. Nothing can be proved, however, so Vin sticks like epoxy to his story.

Then what does Bill Rooney do? From a mile away, he sneaks up on a big buck right in the middle of a herd without one of the antelope spotting him. Up until then I liked Rooney a lot, but I simply cannot tolerate a show-off. To make matters worse, a Wyoming game warden who checked us said it was the best antelope he had seen taken that year!

I thought the worst had to be over, but when we got back to camp, I discovered that Kathy and Bob Etling had each got an antelope. Never have I been on a hunt in which so many things went wrong.

I had been told that antelope are easy to hunt, but I daresay that is not the case. They are cunning beasts. Off in the far distance, streams of them flow hither and yon, waves of them wash across the prairie, and fringes of them decorate almost every ridgeline. Occasionally they will streak, zip, or flash past within rifle range. Not once, however, did I see any antelope play, as is reputed in the song. Show me an antelope playing and I'll show you some antelope chops. Personally, I doubt the songwriter ever even saw an antelope, let alone one that played.

That night as I slouched in a corner of the camper,

with the din of Vin's endless account of his long shot assaulting my eardrums, Kathy Etling slipped over beside me.

"Pat," she whispered, "I saw some dumb antelope today. I know where you can probably get one of them."

Kathy is a very nice person, and I didn't want to let on that there was simply no way I, a sportsman, would take advantage of some poor creature lacking in normal intelligence.

"How dumb, Kathy?"

"Really dumb."

"Well, thanks anyway, but I'm really not interested," I said, patting her on the shoulder. "Just for the heck of it, though, could you draw me a map?"

She drew the map on the back of an envelope, sketching in various landmarks. "How's that?"

"Fine. But I don't see any antelope."

She put an X on the map. "There's one."

You may think I'm exaggerating, Clare, but I'm not. Kathy actually drew the map just as I've described it, right down to the X. Naturally, this is just between you and me, and Kathy, of course. I wouldn't want Sparano or Zumbo to find out about the map, because I would never hear the end of it.

The next day Zumbo, Sparano, and Rooney went out with me on my hunt, each of them offering suggestions as to where I might find antelope. I refused to listen.

"Turn here, by the green post," I told Zumbo. "Turn right after we cross that big culvert. Then drive straight ahead three-quarters of a mile until we come to a large open area with a low ridge off to the south of it."

"You been up here before?" Jim said.

"Nope," I said. "Why do you ask?"

"No reason."

"This is crazy!" Sparano said. "There aren't any antelope around here. An antelope would have to be stupid to be in a place like this."

"Stop here!"

"Here?" Rooney said. "We're right out in the open. Even if there were any antelope here they could see us from a mile away in any direction. But there aren't any antelope here."

I got out, loaded my rifle, and walked a couple hundred feet away from the rig. The little group of observers sprawled out on the ground, sighing, groaning, and occasionally snickering.

After waiting twenty minutes for the arrival of an antelope, I began to wonder if maybe the boys had put Kathy up to drawing the map. It would have been about like them. Still, Kathy didn't seem the type to help perpetrate a low-down, dirty, rotten practical joke, even though it struck me as a pretty good one and probably worth a try on Zumbo sometime.

Suddenly, a dot appeared at the top of the ridge. I put my riflescope on the dot. The dot was staring back at me. It was an antelope, with horns. It sees me, I thought. There's no way it's going to come within range. As if reading my mind, the antelope galloped down off the ridge—*straight toward me!* Incredible! Here, truly, was a dumb antelope! It stopped three hundred yards away, offering an easy target. I fired, kicking up a spout of dust a couple of feet to its right. This, I should mention, is a good way to test an animal's reflexes, but should not be attempted by beginners.

The antelope, displaying excellent reflexes, if a total lack of good judgment, bounded up in the air and took off, turning into one of the brown-and-white streaks for which the species is noted. But it was still streaking right at me! Cool as ice, I stopped its charge with a perfect offhand shot at fifty yards. Indeed, if I had flinched even slightly, I might have hit the befuddled creature, but such was not my intent. I had, of course, perceived that the antelope was not only extraordinarily dumb but also malicious, and dead set on attacking us. For that reason, I had fired a warning shot across its bow and thereby dissuaded it from carrying out its dastardly assault. The antelope, obviously shocked by this impressive display of marksmanship, streaked to safety.

"Wow!" said Zumbo.

"Amazing!" cried Rooney.

"I never saw anything like it!" exclaimed Sparano.

"It was nothing," I responded modestly.

"It was less than nothing!" shouted Zumbo. "An easy shot like that, and you missed? I can't believe it!"

I tried to explain that I had accomplished my intended purpose, but unfortunately my associates chose to cling to their own interpretation of the event. Naturally, I was more than a little annoyed. Here I had just stopped an antelope in midcharge and saved myself and probably them from a bad goring—a pronghorn gore is one of the worst kinds, too. But what thanks did I get? Nothing but ridicule.

"I will admit," Rooney finally admitted, "that it would have been unsportsmanlike to shoot that antelope. It was just too dumb."

"Yeah," agreed Sparano. "The world's dumbest antelope!"

"What a day!" exclaimed Zumbo. "The world's worst shot meets the world's dumbest antelope!"

I hope you won't mind, Clare, but I forged your name to a letter sending Zumbo on assignment to Borneo, where he will be reimbursed for expenses by a fat bald man wearing a white suit with a red carnation in the lapel.

Before I forget, I would like to mention the cowardly behavior of Vin Sparano. Every time I drove our rental rig up to some rugged terrain, a deep gully, a bad stream crossing, or a rickety bridge, Vin would yell, "Wait! Wait! I'd better get out and take a look at this!" Then he would walk across the questionable area and, once he was safely on the other side, signal for me to drive over. I couldn't help but be amused by his use of the old "checking it out" ploy.

You would have expired of mirth, Clare, if you could have seen Vin yelling and hollering and practically hurling himself out the door when we came to one particularly nasty area. The road slanted off at a forty-five-degree angle to the edge of a cliff, which dropped down into a river. Ol' Vin was out there hopping up and down, yelling, "Go back, you fool, go back! You can't make it! You'll slide into the river!"

You should have seen Vin's face when I threw that rental rig into four-wheel-drive and plowed on ahead. Funneeeey!

Oh, I just remembered another item under Miscellaneous on my list of expenses. But more about that later.

Cordially,

Pat

Out of Sync

Over the years I have observed a recurrent failure in the *Homo sapiens* species to get itself in sync. For example, two nations will decide to have a war, and each will send a great army to the wrong place at the wrong time, and they won't be able to find each other. This is enormously embarrassing to the generals, although the troops don't mind, often saying to each other, "Whew-eeee! That was a close one!"

My dictionary defines "sync" as "an act or instance of synchronizing." It defines "synchronizing" as "1. to occur or exist at the same time. 2. to operate at the same rate or simultaneously."

Sync is what I am out of. Always have been, always will be. My fishing and the fish biting, for example, almost never occur or exist at the same time. You would think that during all the years I've spent hunting, I and a trophy elk would show up at the same place at the same time. But that has never happened. As far as I can tell, elk are even more out of sync than I am.

Wonderful sales on outdoor gear occur or exist at the very times a surplus in my bank account does not occur or exist.

In shooting, I have discovered that my shot and the game do not arrive at a given spot at the same time. "I'm just out of sync," I tell my friends. "You're just a bad shot," they reply. My friends know next to nothing about sync.

My fishing buddy Keith Jackson is seriously out of sync, too. For many years, we didn't realize that we were both out of sync, and a good deal of confusion resulted. The most extreme case of this confusion occurred on a fishing trip to the Olympic Peninsula. The first bit of out-of-syncness resulted in our not being able to leave at the same time on the four-hundred-mile drive to the fishing place. I had to leave a day later. Jackson said that was all right. He would haul the boat and have the fish all scouted out by the time I arrived.

He then gave me a complicated set of directions as to the time and place of the rendezvous. "I'll meet you by the brown farmhouse two miles past the dairy at five-thirty in the morning," he said.

"Right," I said.

I drove all night and arrived in the general area of the rendezvous at four in the morning, only to discover that the entire region was saturated with dairies. Furthermore, residual darkness prevented me from determining the color of the houses. I thought about getting out of the car, tiptoeing over to a likely-looking house, and holding a lighted match up next to the siding to determine its color. (Crazy thoughts like that often pop into a fisherman's mind while at peak anxiety over missing a fishing trip.) What gave me pause, however, was the mental image of a farmer coming out of his house, groggy with sleep and irritated at having to milk a bunch of dumb cows who are eating him into bankruptcy, only to find a stranger holding a lighted match to his siding.

"Just checking the color of your house paint," I'd explain.

"Yup," the farmer would say, turning to his great Dane. "Git him, boy."

By five-thirty I was parked in front of a likely looking brown house, one of approximately fifteen brown houses in the area. "Maybe this isn't the right brown house," I said to myself. "Probably it's that brown house I passed two miles back." I then raced off to that brown house. Then I thought of another brown house that had to be the one. And so on. For the next three hours, I drove frantically from one brown house to another. No Jackson.

Meanwhile, Jackson is parked in front of a brown house, frantically watching the minutes of his fishing time tick away. "I'll just bet that stupid McManus is parked in front of the brown house by the old Smith dairy. I'd better go check." He roars off. Five minutes later I arrive at the brown house he just left. Jackson sees that I'm not at the old Smith dairy brown house and roars back to his original brown house, which I have just left to check the brown house at the old Smith dairy. (All this we calmly figured out later, after trying to beat each other with tire irons.)

By eight o'clock Jackson had sunken into a state of blathering insanity, in which condition he was suddenly possessed by the irresistible urge to go fishing without me. Half an hour later, he was trolling alone for salmon in Puget Sound, such was the depth of his madness.

At ten o'clock I gave up on brown houses and drove down to the nearest boat launch. There was Jackson's

pickup and his empty boat trailer. "Why," I said to myself, "that rascal has gone fishing without me." (I'm not
sure "rascal" is the exact word I used, but it will do for
here.) Naturally, I assumed that Jackson never had any
intention of meeting me at a brown house but instead
had just gone fishing. Being a reflective person, I hunk-
ered in the sand and reflected about what to do next.
Letting the air out of all of Jackson's tires seemed to
dominate my reflections, but I decided to give him one
more chance.

Since by now I was starving, I wrote a note saying: "I
have gone to the Singing Salmon Café to eat breakfast."
I put this note on Jackson's windshield. After breakfast,
I drove back to the launch. I parked my car next to his
rig, got out, turned over the note on his windshield, and
wrote, "I am asleep in my car next to your rig."

So Jackson returns from his morning of fishing and
gets in his pickup. He reads the note through his windshield. The note says, "I have gone to the Singing
Salmon Café to eat breakfast." He grabs the note off
the windshield, wads it up, and heads for the Singing
Salmon Café, no doubt intending to give me the thrashing he thinks I so richly deserve for making him miss
three hours of the best fishing time.

I wake up a short while later. Jackson's truck and
trailer are gone! He has deliberately ignored my note!
I now realize that Jackson not only has sent me on a
wild goose chase for a mythical brown house and has
gone fishing without me, he is going to great lengths to
avoid me. I know that he is involved in something he
doesn't want me to know about. He's afraid I'll tattle to
his wife. Ha! What kind of person does he think I am?
I leap in my car and begin the return of the eight-
hundred-mile round-trip, never once having set eye on

Jackson or put lure to water. "Just wait, Jackson," I growl to myself. "Just wait until your wife hears what sort of high jinks you've been up to!"

After that misadventure, Jackson and I realized that we were both hopelessly out of sync with each other. So we worked out a plan. No matter where we intend to meet for a fishing trip, Jackson says, "I'll meet you by the brown farmhouse."

"Right," I say. We now know that it doesn't make any difference what brown farmhouse or where the brown farmhouse is, because we would never arrive at the same time and place anyway. We just go off on our own in- dividual fishing trips. There's about as much chance we'll meet up that way as if we had synchronized for a rendezvous. In fact, probably a better chance.

My whole family has never been in sync about any- thing but particularly in regard to fishing. I recall the time my stepfather, Hank, and my mother had a little spat. Hank was steaming mad, and he told Mom, "Dang it, woman, I'm going down and fish the crick and get myself some peace and quiet!"

"Good!" Mom shouted. "Maybe that will cool you off!"

Hank stormed out of the house, banging the screen door as loudly as he could. Mom sat around seething and speaking ill of Hank. "That old fool! I don't know what I ever saw in him. He's so stubborn and opinion- ated and I don't know what all."

After a bit, however, her rage subsided and she began to think more kindly of Hank. "He's a hard worker, though. I'll say that for him," she said. "I guess he's not so bad."

I thought I'd put in a good word for Hank, to speed reconciliation along. "Yeah, and he's not all that stub- born and opinionated, if you ask me."

"Nobody asked you. If stubborn was hay and opinions were cows, we'd have the biggest farm in the county. What I ever saw in that man, I'll never know!"

"Forget I mentioned it."

By late afternoon, Hank still hadn't returned from fishing. He was getting along in years, and I could tell Mom was sorry about their argument and was beginning to worry about Hank. Then a thunderstorm blew in and rain began to pound down in torrents.

"Oh, good heavens," Mom cried, "poor Hank will get soaking wet. Where could he be? I think I'll drive up to the bridge. If he's there, I can give him a ride home." She rushed out of the house and drove off.

Hank meanwhile was dry and comfortable, sitting under the thick foliage of a huge cedar tree, puffing contentedly away on his pipe and waiting for the storm to pass. The bridge was about two hundred yards away. As he stared vacantly in that direction, he saw Mom drive up in our car, which she turned around and parked on the bridge.

"Aha," he thought. "She has driven out here to pick me up and make amends. She is not such a bad woman after all, even if she is excessively stubborn and opinionated."

Hank then rushed out into the storm, the icy rain plastering his clothes to his body as he galloped along. His lucky fishing hat blew off into the creek. As he grabbed for it, he tripped over a log and fell flat on his face in a mud puddle. Putting off howling with pain and nursing his injured leg until later, he leaped up and fought his way through a thorn thicket, emerging from which he dropped into a drainage ditch, the greenish ooze reaching almost to his armpits. Hauling himself out on a rusty strand of barbwire fence, he punctured random parts of his anatomy on the barbs, but nothing could detain him in his rush toward the car and amends with Mom. Finally, he hurled his torn, bleeding, gasping, freezing body onto the road and limped hurriedly to within three feet of the car's rear bumper, a pained smile of gratitude for Mom's thoughtfulness quivering on his blue lips.

At that moment my mother, seeing no sign of Hank either up or down the creek, calmly drove off. Had she but looked in her rearview mirror, she would have seen a rain-blurred, frenzied figure limping wildly down the road, but Mom didn't believe in rearview mirrors. "There's no point in looking back," she liked to say. "You might see something gaining on you." In this case, the something would have been Hank. Even with a bad leg, the man could move fast, if he was mad enough.

Once Keith Jackson asked me how I had ever got so out of sync. "I inherited the tendency," I said. "Got it from my mother. How about you?"

"Caught it from one of my fishing partners. Anyway, let's go fishing tomorrow. Meet you at the brown house."

"Right," I said. "The brown house."

Kid Brothers and Their
Practical Application

I always thought it would be nice to have a
kid brother. All I ever had was an older sister, who
at best wasn't much fun and at worst was dreadful. It is
a terrible thing to have a sister who is bigger and
stronger than you are. Say you're hanging out in the
yard with some of the guys, explaining to them exactly
what you'll do to the school bully if he "pulls any of that
stuff" with you, and suddenly your older sister comes
out on the porch and bellows at you to get in the house
and help with the dishes. You respond with a cutting
remark that gets a chuckle out of the guys. Your sister
then bounds off the porch, throws three of the guys to
the ground, grabs you, twists your arm up between your
shoulder blades, and marches you into the house on
your tiptoes. That sort of thing can ruin a guy's image.
Older sisters can be bad.

But suppose you had a kid brother, say about three
years younger than yourself. Think of the fun you could
have with him. You could lock him in the basement, say,

and turn off all the lights, and he's down there screaming and yelling and crying, claiming that he just felt an
icy hand on his neck. See, he doesn't know it's your icy
hand, because you sneaked back into the basement and
grabbed him by the neck. And sometimes, when there
wasn't anything else to do, you could practice your tying-
up techniques on him. (Kids realize early on that when
they get to be adults they'll have to spend a lot of time
tying people up, so it's important they get practice. A kid
brother would be perfect for this.) One of the best things
of all you could do with a kid brother would be to say,
"Beat it, kid," whenever he tried to hang out with you
and the guys, and he would have to beat it, because if
he doesn't he knows you'll lock him in the basement again.

You could teach your kid brother all kinds of stuff,
too, just to help him out. You could teach him how
to build a campfire and pitch a tent and bait a hook
and make a slingshot or a bow-and-arrow. Maybe he
wouldn't want to learn any of this stuff, but that wouldn't
make any difference, because he would be smaller than
you, and you could teach him anyway. What's the use
of knowing something if you don't have anybody around
to teach it to?

Whenever you weren't tying him up or locking him
in the basement or teaching him things or telling him
to beat it, you could find lots of other uses for a kid
brother. You could send him on errands, real or imag-
inary, play the old snipe-trapping trick on him, use him
as a test pilot on rafts and go-carts to see if they were
safe, any number of things. I really missed having a kid
brother.

Several of my friends had kid brothers, and more or
less took them for granted. I envied them but never let

on. The accepted attitude toward kid brothers was to regard them as a nuisance. I personally felt that my associates never exploited their kid brothers to the full potential, but I didn't feel it would be appropriate for me to offer advice. That would be like a man who had never owned a dog lecturing his friends on how to train their dogs. (Actually, this is a favorite pastime of persons who have never owned a dog, but why put myself in a bad mood by dwelling on it?) Many was the time when one of my friends complained there was nothing to do that I wanted to suggest we tie up his kid brother in the basement and turn off the lights and listen to him yell. But I never did. It would have been different if I'd had one of my own, so we could have taken turns using each other's kid brother for a project. You take advantage of a person if you can't return the favor in kind, and that's not right.

My friend Retch Sweeney had two kid brothers, Erful and Verman. Erful was about the right age for a kid brother, three years younger than ourselves, and we got quite a bit of use out of him. Verman was too young and small to be of much value. Besides, he had a runny nose all the time, and it made you sick to look at him, let alone to actually touch him. A runny nose is a great defense mechanism if you're a kid brother. Even now it turns my stomach, just remembering little Verman. I thought of him as the Nose.

Erful Sweeney was a chunky toe-head, meaning that he had a head that looked like a toe. I don't know if he was born that way or whether Retch had done the shaping on the kid's head after he was older. To call Erful homely was to flatter him extravagantly.

As a kid brother, Erful seemed just about perfect to

me, but Retch regarded him as a large fat tick embedded in his life. Throughout my youthful association with Retch, Erful stands out in my memory as a constant, lurking presence. In the early years at least, he had a low whining threshold, which could get on a person's nerves. Retch and I would be out in the barn shooting baskets in the haymow, and there would be this background sound of Erful whining, "C'mon, you guys, let me play. If you don't, I'm gonna tell!" This was Erful's power whine—"I'm gonna tell!" Sometimes it would make me laugh right out loud, it was so ludicrous. Retch was usually in such big-time trouble with his folks that Erful's telling on him for not letting him play was like giving a parking ticket to John Dillinger. "Beat it, kid," Retch would say, "before I tie you up in the basement and turn off all the lights."

"Hey, good idea," I'd say.

"I'll tell!" Erful would whine.

Erful had a face that only a mother could love, and I don't think his mother cared all that much for it. She seemed always trying to get his face out of the house.

"Where you boys going now?" she demanded of us one day.

"Down to the river fishin'," Retch said. "And I ain't takin' Erful."

"You most certainly are taking Erful! You just wait until he finishes his peanut butter and jelly sandwich. Erful, hurry up and eat so you can go fishing with Pat and Retch. Wash your toe—uh—your face first."

"C'mon, Ma, don't be mean," Retch said. "Why do I have to take Erful everywhere?"

"Because he's your brother, that's why. Besides, this will give Erful a chance to use the new fish pole he got for his birthday."

"Yeah!" Erful said. "And my new reel! Wow! Wait up, guys, till I go get my new fish pole and reel."

Then Verman piped up, wiping his sleeve across his nose, "Can I go fishin' with Pat and Retch, too, Ma?"

Mrs. Sweeney looked at her youngest son, the Nose. "No, you're—gag—too little to go down to the—gag—river. Then again—gag—maybe not."

We went out and got on our bikes. The standard procedure for the older guys was to ride off as fast as possible and leave the kid brother far behind, whining loudly, "Wait up! You're going too fast!" We always got a chuckle out of this particular whine, since the kid brother obviously thought we were unaware we were going too fast for him. Once out of sight of our pursuer, we would hide and let him race on by, still howling, "Wait up, guys! You're going too fast!" even though we were no longer even in sight. Kid brothers were dumb.

On this particular day, Retch tried to vary the routine a little. Before we rode off from his house, he said to Erful, "Hey, Erful, let's run down to the basement a second. I got some candy hidden away down there. Don't that sound good?"

"Naw," Erful said. "You're not getting me down in the basement! Whine whine."

Usually, Erful wasn't that suspicious. As I told Retch later, the trick might have worked if he hadn't been holding the length of clothesline rope right out where Erful could see it.

All we could do was ride away from Erful, hide until he went whining by, and then go off fishing at some remote place along the river where he wasn't likely to find us, in other words the standard procedure, which was all right but not nearly so efficient as leaving him tied up in the basement.

After we had ditched Erful, Retch and I rode up to China Bend, which was good fishing but a little dangerous, the sort of place where you wouldn't want to fall off the bank or jump in and try to net a fish that was too big just to jerk up onto the bank. Oh, if it was a really big fish, of course you would go in, but it was the sort of risk you wouldn't take for anything under sixteen inches, particularly with the current as cold and churning as it was now.

After a couple of hours, Retch and I had caught half a dozen smallish trout, nothing to get excited about, and were just enjoying the peace and quiet of the river, when all at once Erful came panting up on his bicycle.

"Gee, guys, you lost me," he said. "I guess you wondered what happened to me, but I've been looking all over for you. Bet you thought I went back home."

"Yeah, sort of," Retch said. "When we couldn't find you, we just came up here and started fishin'. I said to ol' Pat here, 'I wonder what became of Erful,' and Pat said, 'Oh, he probably went home.'"

"Nope. I just hunted till I found you. Now I want to try out my new fish pole."

"Yeah, well, this isn't a good place to do it," Retch said. "The bank's startin' to cave away and you might fall in."

"Oh sure, tell me about it!" Erful whined. "You're just tryin' to get rid of me! I'm gonna tell, too!" With that, he stepped over to the edge of the bank, which instantly caved in with him. Shrieking, he clawed at the loosening sod around him, his feet already being swept downstream by the greedy current. Ignoring the impulse to laugh at this comical spectacle, I lunged heroically toward the bank, grabbed Erful by his toe-head, and hauled him to safety. (Later I thought how lucky that it had been Erful the bank had caved in with and not Verman, because the Nose probably would have had to go into the river.)

In all the excitement, it took us several seconds to realize that Erful's new fish pole had plopped right into the deepest hole at China Bend.

"Well, that was one fish pole that didn't last long," Retch said. "Goodbye, birthday fish pole. Maybe next birthday you'll get another one, Erful. That's only a year away. Twelve long months that you'll have to use your old fish pole. I guess you'll pay attention to what I tell you from now on."

Erful emitted a howl of gloom and despair so pitiful that Retch and I had to laugh. He then got on his bike and pedaled off toward home, sounding like a broken fire siren.

"Stupid kid," Retch said, untying the laces on his shoes. "Serves him right, losing his new fish pole." He pulled his sweatshirt off over his head. "I don't know why my folks bother to keep him around." He undid his belt and stepped out of his pants. "He's just a nuisance." Retch then dived into the cold, swirling waters of China Bend.

On his fourth dive, Retch finally found the fish pole and swam downstream to a place where he could claw his way up the bank. He was blue and shivering. He tossed the fish pole on the ground and started putting his pants back on. He didn't say anything for a while, because he was so embarrassed, and also because his teeth were chattering so hard I wouldn't have been able to understand him anyway.

After a bit he said sheepishly, "I hope you won't tell

the guys about this. You know, about me going in the river after Erful's fish pole. It was all he got for his birthday, and . . . "

"Not me," I said. "I'm not going to tell anybody about it."

And I didn't. When you see a character flaw of that magnitude suddenly revealed in your best friend, you're certainly not about to spread it around.

The Fried Flies, Please, and Easy on the Garlic

For some reason I've never been able to comprehend, I sometimes find myself at dinner parties. Startled, I look around and discover that I am seated at a large table with eleven people I've never seen before in my life. This reminds me that I really should pay more attention to where I am going and what I am doing. My goodness, what would I do if I suddenly awoke and found myself in bed with a perfect stranger? With my luck, it would probably be an imperfect stranger, some grizzled, wild-eyed old coot demanding that I check the jug to see if there's another shot of wine left in it. Still, that would be better than finding myself at dinner parties.

Sooner or later, usually sooner, at these dinner parties, the host or hostess will announce, "Mr. McManus hunts, you know." A frigid silence falls over the table like a frozen mute butler, only breaking less china. Soup spoons hang suspended over the vichyssoise.

"Indeeeed!" exclaims a stout matron, sighting down her nose at me.

"Don't start, Martha," mutters a little bald man seated across from her.

Martha starts. "I do hope you won't take offense, Mr. McGinnis, but I view hunters as the lowest form of life, not excluding bacteria and algae."

"No offense taken," I reply, glad for an excuse to ignore my vichyssoise, which I view as the lowest form of food, not excluding lichens and boiled beets.

"I would venture a guess," rumbles a rotund chap dabbing the corners of his prissy lips with a napkin, "that over a lifetime a hunter such as yourself probably has killed dozens of defenseless deer and elk."

"Thank you," I say, politely dabbing vichyssoise off my tongue with my napkin. His estimate is a bit large, but since my hunting companions aren't around to burst into raucous laughter, I let it ride.

Martha now leans forward, her eyes hard and gleaming with anticipation of closing in for the, uh, kill. "So, tell me, Mr. McGillis, and I'm sure all those present will be as interested as I in your response, what is it about killing poor wild creatures that gives you so much sadistic pleasure and satisfaction?"

"Gee, I don't know," I say. "I've always enjoyed killing things. I haven't thought much about it. All I know is, something sets me off and I suddenly have to start killing. One of the things that sets me off is vichyssoise, so I'm sure you'll pardon me if I don't eat any more of it, delicious as it is." I feint playfully at Martha with my butter knife.

"Well," she huffs, "I would certainly never have anything to do with killing."

The main course arrives.

"Oh," cries Martha. "Rack of lamb! One of my favorites!"

"I'm afraid I'll have to pass," I say. "I try to avoid eating anything that died of natural causes. Smells good, though. Is there any chance this lamb could have died in an accident?"

In truth, I've never cared much for killing. There are exceptions. I enjoy killing a big fat housefly that keeps buzzing around my head at night when I'm in bed trying to sleep or read. I leap out of bed, roll up a magazine, and take off after him, trying for wing shots, knocking over lamps and chairs, smashing plaster off the walls, lunging, leaping, diving, trying to get in a mortal wound on my adversary, by which I mean turning him into an amorphous blotch. My wife says she really hates the maniacal laugh that bursts from my drooling and panting lips when I have at last dispatched the cursed fly. She doesn't much like hearing the details of my fly-hunting technique either, such as how you have to lead *behind* a resting fly to get him.

On the other hand, I don't enjoy killing flies that aren't bothering me, flies that are going about their own business, which seems to consist largely of walking up and down windows: "I had a hard day at the office, Maggot. I must have walked up and down that window eighty times and I'm still not done."

Most people, including antihunters, think nothing of killing flies. I think about it. Sometimes my wife says to me, "What are you thinking about?" I tell her, "Killing flies." She usually doesn't ask me what I'm thinking about for several months afterwards, which is good, because usually I'm not thinking about anything. It's embarrassing to be caught thinking about nothing.

I wonder why people should be so unconcerned about

killing a fly and go berserk over the thought of killing a deer.

Is it because flies are more numerous than deer that it's okay to kill them? Of course, people, too, are more numerous than deer, so we'd best avoid that line of reasoning.

Is it because flies aren't as pretty as deer? Most people aren't as pretty as deer, either. If we killed things just because they are ugly, my friend Retch Sweeney would be in big trouble. He wouldn't show his face on the street, I can tell you that.

Maybe some people can't stand the thought of killing deer because deer babies are so cute. Fly babies are about as uncute as it is possible to get. Personally, though, I don't think degree of cuteness should be the deciding factor in whether something is okay to kill. Maybe even fly parents think their babies are cute. Then again, probably not.

Maybe it's okay to kill flies because they are so small. If a thing is small enough, most people aren't bothered much by killing it, which is why ants, aphids, spiders, and all forms of bacteria get so paranoid: "Harry, I tell you I smell Listerine! The fool is going to kill us with Listerine, just because we give him bad breath! I know it, Harry, I tell you I know it!"

Maybe intelligence is the determining factor. I knew a professor once who avoided oysters because, he said, he wouldn't eat anything with that low of an IQ. Flies are pretty smart, though, in my judgment much smarter than oysters and even deer. I don't mean to imply that they would score well on an SAT test. They can't even divide fractions, a characteristic they share with most college graduates. No, I don't think we should say it's all right to kill something merely because of low intelligence. If the ugliness faction didn't get Retch Sweeney, the intelligence faction would. Ole Retch wouldn't be able to step out of his house long enough to snatch the Sunday paper off his porch.

Don't get me wrong. I have no desire to be known as the friend of flies. I'm not going to sponsor a program whereby sportsmen's groups go around putting out rotten garbage for flies during hard winters. I certainly prefer deer over flies, and by a substantial margin, if for no other reason than that deer don't play kickball on a manure pile and then walk around on my potato salad before showering. On the other hand, flies don't eat my fruit trees down to the size of fiddlehead ferns.

I really don't like killing anything, except fat flies maliciously buzzing my head while I'm trying to sleep. But killing is the natural culmination of the pains and pleasures of the hunt, at least if you're a better shot than I am.

Generally speaking, I don't kill anything I don't eat. I draw the line on flies, though. The drumsticks are too small.

At Loose Ends

Give a man enough rope and it will still come
out six inches too short. That is the nature of rope,
if not the nature of man. In fact, the phrase "enough
rope" is deceptive, because there is no such thing as
enough rope. Ask anyone who has tried to tie a canoe
securely to the top of his car.

No driver is more nervous than the one with a canoe
tied to the top of his vehicle. Never mind that he has
bought out the entire rope supply of a hardware store
and his canoe now looks as if it had a gill net draped
over it. Every time he brakes at an intersection, he ex-
pects his canoe to run a red light. This is because the
rope turned out to be six inches too short.

The standard and ideal image of a rope is of a tightly
woven strand of fibers of equal diameter its full length.
Anyone who associates regularly with rope knows that
is not the case. A real rope looks like this: The first two
feet consist of an unraveled portion of hemp leading up
to a big knot whose purpose is to stop the unraveling.

The hemp section, approximately one inch in diameter, contains three other permanent knots of unknown or forgotten function and a permanent loop about the size of a dinner plate. Tied onto the hemp section is a length of semirotten clothesline. This in turn joins a stiff blue nylon water-skiing rope, with the handgrip still attached. The water-skiing section is tied to a length of twine, which serves as the terminal or tie-down end. This is the rope you use to tie a twelve-hundred-dollar canoe to the top of your car. It is six inches too short.

A thorough knowledge of knots is essential to anyone associating with rope on a regular basis. I learned most of my knot-tying during a stint I served as a Cub Scout. Mostly what we did at the Cub Scout meetings was learn to tie knots. True, we were mildly interested in knots, but what we really wanted to learn was how to build fires.

"No, no, boys," the den mother would say nervously. "Tie your knots and then we'll have cocoa and cookies." Mrs. Slocum herself did not know how to tie knots. If she needed a knot tied, she hired someone to do it. Our only source of knot-tying instruction, therefore, was the *Boy Scout Handbook*. The way you tied a bowline, for example, was to follow this sequence: "The rabbit comes out of its hole, goes around the tree, and back into its hole." Then you would pull both ends of the rope tight and the bowline would disappear. Anytime you wanted a knot that disappeared when tightened, you tied a bowline. It's one of the best knots to know.

Our favorite knot was the hangman's. This was one of the few useful knots omitted from the *Boy Scout Handbook*, which is surprising, since the handbook at that time was intended to train youngsters to become adept outdoorsmen. Although the handbook failed to mention it, few things are more annoying to an outdoorsman than when, wet, tired, and hungry, he has to figure out how to tie a hangman's noose after the camp cook has served only boiled beets for dinner. We Cubs fashioned several respectable-looking hangman's knots, much to the dismay of Mrs. Slocum, who always rushed in with cocoa and cookies before we could run any field tests. The woman was all frayed nerves.

The most useful knot was the plain old granny, which has a reputation for slipping. The slipping problem can be solved merely by piling one granny on top of another (not unlike a football scrimmage at an old folks' home) until the sheer weight of the knot holds it in place. I personally still favor the granny over all other knots, although, for safety's sake, I never tie one that weighs less than half a pound or about the size of your average grapefruit. But my knots stay tied. My old friend Crazy Eddie Muldoon will sign an affidavit to the truth of this statement.

When we were about ten years old, Eddie, who lived on the farm next to ours, came over to play one day. He said he had strict orders from his mom to be home in an hour. Otherwise he would be in big trouble.

"Ah, you can stay longer," I said.

"Nope, I can't," Crazy Eddie said. "Ma cut a switch about six feet long and said she'd wear it down to the size of a toothpick on me if I wasn't home by four sharp."

"In that case," I said, "let's play tying up." Tying up was one of our favorite games. It consisted of one person tying the other one up and seeing how long it took him to get loose.

"Okay, I'll go first," Crazy Eddie said. "I been thinking of a new way to tie you up. Ain't no way you're gonna get loose, unless you beg me to untie you."

Eddie used about forty feet of clothesline rope to tie me up but came out six inches too short. That was why it took me only half an hour to wiggle free. "Now it's my turn," I said. "Step over here, Eddie." I pointed to a cast-iron frame that had formerly served as the base for a wood-burning heater but had obviously been intended for tying someone up to. I had Eddie lie down in the middle of the frame and tied each of his hands and legs to one of the four corners with my compound granny knots.

Eddie grunted and struggled but couldn't get loose. Minutes passed. Eddie got angrier and angrier. "This is unfair!" he yelled.

"No, sir," I said. "There's nothing in the rules that says you can't use a cast-iron frame to tie up with." Actually, the only thing in the rules was that you couldn't tickle a guy or otherwise torment him while he was tied up. Because of that limitation, I became bored watching Eddie trying to get loose. I went in the house and made myself a sandwich. By the time I got back, Eddie was seething with rage.

"When I get loose, I'm going to break all your arms and legs three or four times apiece!" he yelled. Up to that point, I had been thinking about untying him. Now I saw that would be unwise and a definite threat to my health. Four o'clock came and went. I began to wish Eddie would get loose on his own, while I stood off at a safe distance, because there was no way for me to untie him without considerable risk to my arms and legs. Time marched on. I got out my jackknife and started whittling sticks to calm my nerves.

"Okay, okay, I give up," Eddie finally said. "Untie me."

"Promise not to break my arms and legs?"

"Yeah."

"Uncross your fingers," I said, because that canceled out any promise.

"Okay."

I rushed over and tried to untie the granny knots. They wouldn't come undone. The only thing to do was to cut the rope, which I did. Eddie rubbed the circulation back into his wrists and ankles. Then he leaped up and threw a half nelson around my neck.

"You promised," I croaked.

"I had my toes crossed."

At that moment, Eddie's mom came around the corner of the house. She was carrying the six-foot-long willow switch. "You're two hours late, young man!" she snarled. "Now march for home!"

"But Ma . . . !" yelled Eddie.

"No buts! March!"

"See ya, Eddie," I said.

I watched Eddie and his mom cross the field to their house. Every four or five steps, I would see Eddie bound into the air. A half second or so later, I would hear the sizzle of the switch and Eddie go "YIPE!" How interesting, I thought. Why shouldn't the sizzle of the switch and the "Yipe!" occur at the same time Eddie bounded into the air? While I was contemplating this curiosity with typical scientific detachment, however, my own mother discovered her clothesline had been cut into a dozen pieces. She began casting about for a suitable switch. This in turn reminded me of my plan to join up with the French Foreign Legion, and I immediately set off in search of a recruiting office. The Foreign Legion always had need of recruits who were good at tying up.

Tying things now seems to be an activity of the distant past. I remember when store clerks routinely wrapped purchases in paper, zapped some string around them from a big spool, and broke off the end with a flick of the wrist and a crisp, satisfying *pop* that signaled the completion of the transaction. Package tying was a craft by which the professional clerk could be recognized. When you got home, all your purchases were neatly wrapped and tied, and you had added to your supply of string for tying up other things around the house. But no more. Now when you get home from shopping all you have is a plastic bag with your purchases lumped in the bottom of it. No string. If you want string, you have to go out and buy it. It's sad. When I was a boy, entire lives were held together with free string. Now everyone seems to be at loose ends!

Perhaps there is no better indication of the demise of tying than the modern pickup truck. Have you recently—by recently, I mean the last thirty years—tried to tie anything down in the bed of a pickup? It's impossible. There is nothing to tie to.

One of the reasons there is nothing to tie to is that pickup designers have discovered that most people no longer actually carry things in their pickups, because the paint might get scratched. I am not of the paint-scratch-fretting school. I still carry things in the bed of my pickup. The other day I went out to a junkyard and bought an old refrigerator that I plan to turn into an old refrigerator. I had taken along some rope to tie the refrigerator down in the pickup bed. (This is a precaution I take ever since I had a washer/dryer combo topple out of the truck on a steep hill and almost rinse and spin-dry a jogger.) The only way I could tie the old refrigerator down was to wrap the rope all the way around under the body of the pickup and up the other side, where it turned out to be six inches too short.

"You don't have enough rope," the junk man said.

"What's new?" I said. "There's no such thing as enough rope."

"True," he said, for he was a man who knew rope. "I guess I'll have to sell you some baling wire to finish the job."

"Baling wire!" I exclaimed. "That's wonderful! I haven't come across any baling wire in years."

"Know why?"

"It's an antique now? A collector's item?"

"You got it, pal. But I can let you have a couple of pieces for, oh, say, five dollars."

"Try saying fifty cents."

"Fif . . . fif . . . fif. Guess I can't say it. I can say 'two dollars,' though."

"Sold."

Naturally, I couldn't use a valuable antique to tie down an old refrigerator. So I made do with what was handy. You don't really need to wear a belt and shoestrings while you're driving. On the other hand, I now wish I had just cinched up the buckle and not added a granny knot. It looks odd with a three-piece suit.

Getting It in the Ear

One of the more interesting things that can happen to an angler is to get a barbed hook sunk into his hide. Such is the horror and fascination of the experience that many an angler has contemplated giving up his regular work and hitting the lecture circuit to entertain audiences around the nation with a dramatic rendering of his ordeal.

Listening to someone tell of being hooked can be a trying experience. Often have I observed a group of my friends listening to a fellow angler relate the grisly details of the extraction of a barbed hook from some valued and sensitive part of his anatomy. I can testify to the looks of disbelief, horror, and revulsion, the gasps and groans. The listeners, on the other hand, are usually bored stiff.

Sport fishing has now been in vogue for several hundred years, during which time the removal of barbed fishhooks from the hides of humans has acquired its own history. During the early days, when the lord of the manor hooked himself, he would select one of his serfs to remove the hook. Generally speaking, serfs did not look upon this as a plum assignment. The serf would grasp the shank of the hook, brace both his feet on the lord, and pull for all he was worth. The method was simple and direct but raised the mortality rate of serfs significantly. Sometimes two or three serfs would be expended in the removal of a single hook.

The twentieth century finally arrived with its advances in medicine and technology, and just in time, too, because the supply of serfs had been pretty well exhausted. Fishing partners could now remove hooks from each other right on the lake or stream, thanks to a new invention: rusty pliers. The technique consisted of grasping the shank of the hook with the pliers, bracing both feet on the hookee, and pulling. The pliers did away with much of the discomfort the extractor of the hook formerly suffered from finger cramps. The invention of ear plugs also reduced the threat of hearing loss that formerly accompanied the hook-removal process.

Then a man known only as Earl devised a procedure for removing hooks that appeared promising. Earl advised twisting the hook in such a manner that the point and the barb were forced up through the skin of the angler. The barb could then be clipped off and the rest of the hook easily removed. He demonstrated this technique on a burly young man by the name of Bubba, and narrowly escaped with his life. Earl now lives in a different town under an assumed identity. His technique, however, became widely accepted among anglers. It can be safely applied with nothing more than a pair of rusty pliers, a stout chair, and, depending on the size of the hooked angler, ten to fifteen feet of good rope.

Getting hooked invariably leads to an instant social

occasion. The reason for this is that one's fishing partners feel that an audience for the hook removal will inhibit the hookee from extreme emotional outbursts. Even as great chunks of his flesh are gouged out of him—"great chunks" meaning any the size of a pinhead or larger—the angler will stoically sit there telling jokes: "Then there was the one about the chicken and the turtle—OWWW!—and so anyway the rabbit is— OWWW!—well, the farmer comes home right then and—OWWW!" That is why as soon as someone is hooked, one of his companions must leap to his feet and announce to all the fishermen within a quarter mile, "Hey, we got a man hooked here!"

It so happens that every fisherman ever born has developed his own theory for hook removal. Here, now, is his chance to test the theory on someone besides himself. Upon the announcement that a man has been hooked, all boats on a lake will immediately converge on the scene of the disaster. If the hooking occurs on a stream, men, women, and children will come running from all directions, some charging right through boiling rapids in their effort to arrive in time and foist off their theory on the attending "surgeon," usually a man known only as Earl.

There is a good deal of pushing and shoving as the assembled anglers struggle with each other to get their hands on the offending hook and test their particular theory. Everyone is shouting opinions and recommending techniques: "Best way to do that . . . Twist and pull real hard . . . Take a sharp knife and . . . Tie a string between the hook and the anchor and . . . "

After a while the anglers begin swapping tales about the times they got hooked and how much worse hookings they were than the one here being witnessed. Beverages and sandwiches are broken out, and a full-scale party is soon under way. Hookings are to fishermen what barn-raisings were to the pioneers, an opportunity for socializing in an otherwise solitary enterprise.

I myself have been hooked only twice in my life. On the first occasion, Retch Sweeney and I were fishing from a bass boat. Our motor had conked out, and we were faced with the prospect of having to paddle the boat all the way across the lake to the launch area. The wind had come up, and as I was making my final cast, a gust whipped my line around me and I buried the hook in the flab of my left side. Retch took charge, delighted to have this opportunity to test one of his many theories for hook removal.

As soon as he had shouted out the requisite, "Hey, we have a man hooked here!" (even though we were the only ones on the lake), he cut away my shirt, pleased with the chance to use his new knife, grabbed a pair of rusty pliers, and began worrying the hook, although a good deal less than me. Frustrated in his effort, he fell back on the traditional tactic of bracing both feet on the hookee and pulling, thereby stretching my flab out in the vague shape of a sail. The wind caught my flab like a jib and began moving us in the general direction of the launch ramp. Retch was all for maintaining this arrangement, because if the wind held and he could tack to the starboard, it would save us a good deal of paddling. I argued against it. The maneuver, however, had loosened the hook, and it dropped out of its own accord. Nevertheless, I do not favor this method and cannot in good faith recommend it. On the plus side, the mishap improved my casting fourfold, and fifteen years passed before I hooked myself again.

The second and most recent hooking occurred while I was fishing with my irascible neighbor, Alphonse P.

Finley. Finley was winding up for a cast when I suddenly had the sensation that one of my ears had been turned into live bait. Apparently unaware that he had hooked me, Finley attempted to cast my ear into a patch of lily pads and might well have succeeded if the ear had been less firmly attached to my head. I immediately called Finley's attention to the problem. Startled, he looked around. "Cripes!" he said. "I thought Jaws III had taken a bite out of you! And all it is, you've got a set of treble hooks dangling from your ear. Where's my rusty pliers? I've got a surefire technique for removing hooks from ears. But first, let me say this."

"What?"

"Hey, we've got a man hooked over here!" he shouted.

Once again I was saved the ordeal of an audience, Finley and I being the only anglers on the lake.

"Forget your technique," I said. "I'm having a doctor remove this hook! Now just get your clippers and snip the line from the hook."

Always one for taking a bad situation and making it worse, Finley looked around for his clippers, backed up, and bumped against my head—sinking one of the treble hooks all the way through his sweatshirt! My ear was now firmly attached to Finley's back just above his beltline.

"You'll have to take your sweatshirt off," I said.

"I can't," Finley said. "The hook went through my long underwear too."

"Well, if you can't pull the sweatshirt over your head, see if you can't wiggle out through the neck."

Finley wiggled and squirmed, grunted and groaned. "No, I can't make it," he said in a strangled voice. "Now I've got my arm stuck straight up through the neck of the sweatshirt and can't get it back in!"

"This is the worst predicament I've ever been in," I

said. "Somehow we've got to get this boat back to shore, get into your car, drive to that gas station down the road, and have the attendant cut us loose."

"I have some more bad news for you," Finley said.

"What?"

"I've got to go to the bathroom."

An hour later, we pulled into the gas station. Carefully, we eased out of the car, with me cheek to cheek with Finley's backside, and Finley with his arm sticking straight up out of the neck of his sweatshirt. Three old codgers, tilted back in their chairs against the station, watched us curiously, apparently unaccustomed to seeing strangers in those parts.

Finley, no doubt directing a strained smile at them, croaked, "Would one of you gentlemen be kind enough to direct me to the men's restroom, or the ladies', for that matter, whichever is unoccupied at the moment?"

"Wait! Stop!" I shouted. "Someone cut us loose first!"

The codgers came over for a closer look. "Dad gum, I see the problem," one of them said. "They's hooked together with fishhooks. At first I thought you fellers was just from New York City. Hey, Ben, bring me them wire snippers."

In a few seconds, we were snipped apart, and none too soon, for Finley homed in on the men's room like a heat-seeking missile. While I stared after Al, contemplating the peril I'd narrowly escaped, the old codger who had snipped us apart tugged at the lure dangling from my ear.

"Let me have a go at the hook in your ear," he said. "I got a special technique for gettin' hooks out of ears."

"Why not?" I said. "Okay, have at it, Mr. . . . Mr. . . . "

The old gent smiled and pulled a rusty pair of pliers from his hip pocket. "Just call me Earl," he said.

Garage-Sale Hype

Ninety-eight percent of all hunting and fishing time is spent getting ready to go hunting and
fishing. Getting ready consists primarily of buying stuff.
The easiest place to buy the stuff is at a sporting goods
store, which has the disadvantage of fixed prices. Often,
however, you can find just what you're looking for at a
garage sale, where, if you don't mind haggling a bit, you
can get a used item for scarcely more than you would
pay for a new one. Furthermore, fish and game laws in
all fifty states permit you to refer to any sporting gear
bought at a garage sale as "a terrific bargain." If the item
proves to be defective, you can always return it to the
operator of the garage sale, and he will happily return
your money, but only if you can provide identification
proving you are a recent escapee from a maximum-
security prison for the criminally insane.

I myself am a skilled garage-sale shopper. Whenever
I'm looking for a real bargain on some outdoor gear, I
buy the first edition of the Sunday newspaper Saturday

evening. That gives me an edge on the other bargain hunters who might scan the classified ads in the later editions for the same neat stuff I'm after.

Last Saturday evening I was sitting in my study (also known as the laundry room) perusing the classified section of the Sunday paper when my irritable neighbor, Al Finley, burst in on me.

"Darn it, Finley!" I said. "Knock before you come charging into somebody's house. You startled me."

"Good!" Finley snapped. "Besides, I did knock."

"You did? I guess I didn't hear you because the washing machine was running. Anyway, when I didn't answer your knock you should have realized I wasn't home and gone away."

I knew, of course, that Finley had come over to borrow back some of his tools. I really wouldn't mind loaning him his tools so much if he would just take better care of them and return them promptly.

"I need my electric drill back. Let's go get it! Right now!" he pleaded, tugging playfully on my ear.

"Okay, okay," I said. "Just wait until I finish checking the ads for garage sales. Whoa! What's this? Retch Sweeney is holding a garage sale tomorrow. Mostly outdoor gear. Rods, reels, assorted fishing tackle, his old pump shotgun with the bent barrel, a bunch of other stuff. What say we beat it over to his house, or rather his garage, and jump on some bargains before the other bargain hunters show up tomorrow?"

"That elbow!" (Finley has the habit of applying crude anatomical names to people he doesn't like.) "What would I want with any of his junk?"

"Well, you did lose that spinning reel over the side of the boat last week. Maybe you can pick up another one at a bargain price at Retch's garage sale."

"Oh yeah? You're the one who'd better pick up another reel for me, preferably at a *new* price. It was you who dropped it over the side of the boat. I wasn't even fishing with you!"

"Let's not quibble over meaningless details," I said, grabbing my jacket off the clothes hamper. "We'd best get over to Retch's garage just in case some premature shoppers scarf up all the good stuff."

"Much as I hate to admit it, that might not be a bad idea," Finley said.

"Darn right," I said. "We'll take your car. It'll be better that way."

"Why is it better that we always take my car?"

"It's just better, that's why. Do I constantly have to explain everything to you, Finley?"

"Ye gads!"

The light was still on in Retch's garage, and there was no sign of other bargain hunters lurking about. Retch was arranging some of his sale items on top of his Ping-Pong table and another table he had made out of a sheet of plywood and a couple of sawhorses. Boxes of tattered, torn, worn, rusty, bent, battered, and broken items of outdoor gear were lined up along the walls. There were snowshoes, empty shell casings, rods, reels, assorted fishing lures, a couple of landing nets, a canoe paddle, a rubber raft, three outboard motors, and a few hundred other items heaped in random piles about the garage.

"Wow!" I said. "This is quite a sale."

"Yeah," Retch said, stepping back to examine the arrangement he had been working on. "I figure I'll sell enough to buy that bass boat I've been looking at."

Finley snorted. "You silly elbow, you think somebody is actually going to pay money for this conglomeration of dismal junk? You've got to be kidding!" He poked gingerly at a rusty old tackle box.

"Careful with the merchandise, Finley," Retch said. "You break it, you've bought it."

"Aha, I see you've already picked up the lingo of marketing. But it's going to take a lot more than lingo to sell this detritus."

"Detritus? That's a tackle box—an antique tackle box! Cripes, don't you even know an antique tackle box when you see one? Anyhow, it might just interest you to know, Finley, that I am a master of sales psychology. A lot of guys that show up at a garage sale, all they plan on doing is looking. Oh, sure, if you got a dirt-cheap price on something they want, maybe then they'll buy it. But then I lay the old psychology on them, and before they know it they're walking out of here with an armload of merchandise."

Finley chuckled. "Psychology! I suspect you know about as much psychology as a mollusk."

"Well, maybe I do and maybe I don't. It just depends."

"Depends on what?"

"On what a mollusk is. Okay, Finley, you think you're so smart, I'll just give you an example of how to send a bargain hunter into a buying frenzy. Now the first thing you do is price everything up real high. Say about triple what you figure something is worth. That gives you a margin for haggling, should it come to that. Of course, you don't mark the prices on anything—you keep them in your head. So in comes a guy and he's kinda sniffing over your stuff, thinking you're gonna ask an arm and a leg for everything. So he picks up a nice little reel, for instance, and he figures if he haggles real hard he can get it for maybe ten bucks. He says, 'How much you askin' for this battered-up old reel?' I says, real dumb-

like, 'Gosh, I don't know. How does two dollars sound?'
Well, his ol' eyeballs light up and start dancing around
over the rest of my merchandise like he's finally struck
the mother lode of garage sales. 'How much you want
for them snowshoes?' he yells. I says, 'Oh, gosh, I guess
fifty bucks would . . . And he yells, 'I'll take 'em! How
much you want for . . . ?' Before you know it, he's got
a bunch of my jun—uh, merchandise, and I got all his
money. See, I've suckered the poor bugger right into a
buying frenzy without him even knowing it. But here's
the tricky part. Every time he asks me a price, I yawn,
just like I'm so bored with the deal I can hardly stay
awake. Works like a charm!"

Finley looked at me. "Can you believe this nonsense?
Buying frenzy! Garage-sale hype! Now I've heard it all!"

"You ain't heard it all, Finley," Retch said. "There's
a whole lot more, but this ain't no seminar for your
personal education in how to operate a garage sale. Besides, I got work to do. Come back tomorrow and I'll
give you a demonstration of buying frenzy."

"I may just do that," Finley said. "Garage-sale psychology! Ha!"

"Yeah, me too," I said. "I may come to observe your
technique. I've got a bunch of jun—uh, used items that
I wouldn't mind unload—uh, selling. I find it kind of
hard to believe, though, that someone would actually
fall for this malarkey."

"He's out of his mind," Finley said, flipping shut the
lid of the tackle box and blowing the rust off his fingers.
"There's no way anyone old enough to be out alone
without his mother would fall for any of this elbow 'psychology.' I would . . . " Finley suddenly nudged me in
the ribs.

"Look over there on the Ping-Pong table," he whispered. "That reel! It's just like the one of mine you dropped out of the boat, you kneecap. That was a forty-dollar reel. Now's your chance to replace it. The elbow probably wants eighty for it."

"Yeah, you're probably right," I said. I walked over and picked up the reel. "How much you asking for this old beat-up spinning reel, Retch?"

"That old thing?" he said, scratching his head and yawning. "Oh, I don't know. How does two dollars sound?"

Finley chuckled all the way home. He even let me drive his car, so he could concentrate on his chuckling. "I can't get over the elbow and his 'sales psychology.' Sometime I'd like to put on a disguise and sneak into one of his garage sales and let him try to pull that stuff on me. I could hardly contain myself when he yawned after you asked the price of the reel. Two bucks! Now, that is, if I do say so myself, a bargain—a reel bargain! Get it? Look. It's just exactly like my reel. I had my initials scratched on it right here, where it has the initials A.F., which happen to be my initials too, and *this is my reel!*"

"Yeah, Finley," I said, "I meant to mention that. You see, after I dropped your reel over the side of the boat, Retch stripped off all his clothes and dove down and retrieved it off the bottom. But when I asked for it back, he claimed salvage rights. That's probably why he let us have it for two bucks. Just to be nice. Thanks, by the way, for loaning me the two bucks. Don't let me forget to pay you back." We both had a good laugh over that zinger.

"I'm just happy to get the reel back," Finley said. "Say, the snowshoes are poking me in the back of the head. Couldn't we put them in the trunk?"

"Nope, trunk's full. Last thing I could squeeze in was the antique tackle box."

"How about on top of the car? We could tie them to the Ping-Pong table."

"Naw, we got too much stuff up there already."

Finley started chuckling again. "I can't get over the elbow and his garage-sale psychology! I'll tell you one good thing about his operation, though."

"What's that?"

"He takes credit cards."

How to Get Started
in Bass Fishing

Many people think they can start fishing for bass just anytime they please and pick up the techniques as they go along. They are right, of course, but in the process they will miss many of the important nuances so important to the sport. Also, they will learn many bad habits and get themselves in embarrassing situations, most of which can be avoided by following the advice set forth below.

You should first buy (note: "buy" is an important and frequently repeated term in the bass angler's technical vocabulary, so learn to pronounce it properly) several essential tools and materials. These are, in order of importance, a hammer, saw, nails, paint, shingles, and a bunch of boards. Once you have everything assembled, begin building an addition onto your house. You will need this addition to store all your bass tackle in. Do not make the mistake of thinking you can simply keep your tackle in an extra bedroom or scattered about the living room, unless you are a bachelor or wish soon to become one. Build the addition.

Now that your addition is built, it is time to go tackle shopping. Go down to your local tackle shop and buy everything in sight. You will eventually end up with all of it anyway, so you might as well get it over with. Put the tackle in your new addition. If there is any left over, store it in an extra bedroom or scatter it about the living room.

Among the stuff you will have bought are things called tackle boxes, which are nothing more than boxes in which you keep tackle. Do not confuse tackle boxes with tackle boxing, which is a form of combat used to decide who gets to use the last lure that is the only thing catching fish. Also, tackle boxes should not be confused with fishing tackle, an extreme maneuver used to prevent a companion from getting to the next fishing hole before you do.

You will notice right away that the tackle boxes are divided up into little sections, which allow you to keep your tackle organized according to kind, size, color, etc. Pay no attention to the little sections. Just grab handfuls of tackle and stuff the boxes full. Since the contents of your tackle boxes will be in a big mess after your first fishing trip anyway, this shortcut will save you a great deal of time. (Millions of hours of fishing time are wasted each year by anglers needlessly organizing their tackle boxes before each trip. Don't fall into this trap.) Now, once the tackle is stuffed into the boxes, you may find ends of plastic worms and line sticking out. Clip these off. Bass fishermen should be neat.

Next, you must begin learning the names of all the stuff you bought. Say that you happen to be the only person to catch a fish in three hours or so. Other bass anglers will pull up next to your boat and say, "What did you catch it on?" If you don't know the name of your lure, all you can say is something like "A little green wiggly thing." The other fishermen will laugh and poke fun at you, while frantically sorting through their tackle boxes for little green wiggly things. It can be embarrassing. Think how much better it will be if you can reply to your inquisitors, "I caught it on a Mister Twister Chartreuse Flake Double Tail." Yes, I know it's difficult to say. That's why you must begin practicing right now.

In learning the names of your tackle, you probably should start with plastic worms. Your basic worms have simple enough names: Black, Purple, Blue, Red, etc. Eventually, though, you will want to move up to your power worms: Smoke, Motor Oil, Black Grape, and Amber Flake. You may think those names are more appropriate to members of a street gang than to plastic worms. The names were in fact borrowed from members of a street gang, who took up bass fishing and went straight. These plastic worms are terrific fish-getters. A bass will start to nibble on Motor Oil and Amber Flake will sneak up behind and mug him. It's a good idea, however, not to be caught alone in the dark with more than six of these power worms. You never know. They may claim you looked like a bass.

Once you have learned all the names of all your fishing tackle, which shouldn't take longer than two years, you are ready to go out on the water and start looking for bass. The first thing you will discover is that bass are very hard to see, because they are covered up with water. This may strike you as taking unfair advantage, as it does me, but that is the way the contest is played. To the inexperienced eye, all water looks pretty much the same. Consequently, you will spend a great deal of time casting your lures into water in which your average bass wouldn't be caught dead. So what do you do?

I recommend that you find an experienced bass fisherman to take you out and instruct you on the fine points of catching bass. My first bass mentor was a chap by the name of Retch Sweeney. On the first day of instruction, he took me to a spot where I would never have guessed a bass might be hanging out. "I bet you would never guess a bass would be hanging out here," he said. "Well, just you cast your Yellow Skirt, Yellow Twister Tail into that brush by the shore and I'll show you something." I made ten or fifteen casts with the spinner bait. "See?" Retch said. "A bass would never hang out here. Let this be a lesson to you." In this way, I quickly learned all the places in our area where not to fish for bass, and also that I had better find another bass-fishing instructor.

My next instructor was a man by the name of Smokey Joe. Smokey taught me a great deal about terminology, particularly what words to use when you jerk your lure off of what you think is the grasp of a submerged log but turns out to be the grasp of a submerged bass the size of a log. Some anglers will respond to this situation by shaking their heads and calmly commenting, "Gosh, a funny thing just happened. I jerked my line because I thought I was hooked up on a log and it was the biggest bass I ever saw in my life. Well, that's the way it goes." Never again go fishing with a bass angler who responds in this way. He is not cut out for the sport and will be a bad influence on you.

Smokey Joe showed me how to respond properly to the log/bass situation. As he snapped the lure free and the monstrous bass thrashed briefly through Smokey's field of vision, he dropped his rod and reel into the boat.

Then he leaned forward, grasping the gunnels with both hands, his eyeballs protruding only slightly in the direction of the empty water through which the bass had churned a moment before, as if the sheer intensity of his stare might bring the bass back. All this while, Smokey was noisily sucking air, expanding his lungs until his shirttails were drawn right out of his grimy jeans. I then saw the reason for his gripping the gunnels, because he began to jump up and down with both feet, and his grasp on the gunnels prevented him from flying out of the boat. (I recognized this as an important tip, and made a mental note to remember just how it was done.) He then used the air in his lungs to power a long, quavering scream of anguish that echoed up and down the lake, and for miles away fishermen said to each other, "Smokey Joe must have lost a trophy bass he thought was a log." At last the scream dribbled out into ominous silence, and I wondered what Smokey would do next. I hoped it didn't involve me. I was relieved to see him sucking air once more, and I wondered if it was for another scream, even though I thought he had exhausted all possibilities for a scream in his first effort. But he didn't scream again. Instead, he moved into the terminology stage, employing exotic words I had never heard before, occasionally and deftly working in the terms "bass" and "log," but they were so burdened down with adjectives it was difficult to notice them. When he reached full pitch, I figured we could have turned off the electric motor and powered the boat at trolling speed with nothing more than Smokey's torrent of terminology. At peak volume, it probably achieved thirty-five pounds of thrust, perhaps more. I realized then that I would need several more years of bass fishing to achieve anything comparable.

When we finished fishing for the day, we pulled in to the dock. Some other anglers were just going out. "Any luck?" one of them asked.

"Caught a few," Smokey said. "And I lost the biggest bass I ever saw in my life."

"Gee, that's too bad," the man said.

Smokey shrugged and smiled. "That's the way it goes."

I knew then that there were nuances to bass fishing that I had never even suspected.

As the Worm Squirms

I was up at my cabin the other day, when young Lonnie Bird stopped by to show me a seven-pound bass he had just caught in the river. A s-e-v-e-n--p-o-u-n-d bass! Never had I seen such a bass taken out of the river, the very same river that for twenty years I had beaten to a froth from mouth to source with every lure known to man and never landed a bass over two pounds. My head reeled at the sight of the thing. From *my* river! A *SEVEN-POUND* BASS! I had to force myself to breathe. My whole life as an angler flashed before my eyes, and I thought I must surely be dying from the mere sight of this finny miracle.

"Not a bad fish, Lonnie," I said. "Where'd you catch him?"

"Up in Crawford Slough. You know where those submerged stumps are at the head of the slough?"

Crawford Slough! Cripes! The submerged stumps! Oh, the pain! I can't stand the pain of it! "Uh-hunh. Crawford

Slough. Well, you got yourself a pretty nice fish there, Lonnie. Probably caught it on a crank bait, right?"

"Nope, a worm."

A worm! Of course! Why didn't I think of that? Aaaaiiii! "Yes, I've found that some of the larger bass will go for a worm this time of year. I bet it was a purple silver-flaked worm with a gray tail. Right?"

"Nope. A real worm."

"What do you mean, a real worm?"

"I mean a real worm, one that ain't plastic."

"Aha! The kind of worm that you dig . . . "

"Yeah, the kind that you buy in the little round paper cartons out of the dairy food section at the Super Mart."

"Oh, that kind of real worm. Well, to tell you the truth, Lonnie, I feel it's much more sporting to use artificial worms. I would have to be pretty hard up for bass before I would resort to fishing with live worms I bought out of the dairy section at the Super Mart."

"Won't do you no good to rush in there after a carton of them, because I bought the last of the Super Mart's worms this morning. The early bird gets the worms! Ha! Get it?"

"Yeah, I get it, you glutton, you hoarder of worms! Listen, I'll give you a buck for a dozen worms right now, no questions asked."

"Nope. By the time the worm man comes around to the Super Mart again, I'll have caught all the seven-pound bass out of Crawford Slough!"

"Okay, Lonnie, I'll show you. I'll just go dig my own worms."

"Dig your own? What do you mean, dig your own? You think worms just grow in the ground? Worms come in round paper cartons from big worm ranches. Everybody knows that. Shoot, if you could just dig 'em out of the ground, the worm man would go bust."

As soon as Lonnie had departed with his monstrous bass, I grabbed a shovel and spaded up an acre of ground. Not a single worm put in an appearance.

The following week I was waiting at the Super Mart for the worm man to bring in a fresh shipment. A late-model pickup truck drove up and a tall, lanky gentleman got out. He was wearing cowboy boots, a ten-gallon hat, and a nice leather vest. He lifted a crate of little round paper cartons from the back of the pickup.

"You must be the worm man," I said.

"Actually, I prefer to be known as a worm rancher," he said frostily.

"I'm sorry," I said. "I should have known—the boots, the hat. How big's your ranch?"

"Almost half an acre."

"Half an acre," I said. "Well, I suppose you can raise quite a few worms on half an acre."

"Yep. Right now I'm runnin' three hundred thousand head on the north pasture alone."

"Wow! How big's the north pasture?"

"About this big, give or take a couple of inches. Most of the stock's out on the open range, though. You might like to come out and watch the roundup."

"A roundup! How many hands does it take for a roundup?"

"Six usually. Mine, my wife's, and my son Grover's."

"Sounds exciting," I said. "It would be worth the trip just to see the itty-bitty branding iron. For right now, though, I'd just like to buy some worms off you."

"Shore thing, podner. How many you want?"

"Oh, about fifty head."

While the worm rancher was counting out my purchase, I started wondering whatever happened to regular old worms, the kind you dig out of the ground rather than out of the dairy case at a grocery store—ranch-raised worms. I'll admit that I'm glad to see the resurgence of worms, whatever their source. For a while, I thought they might have disappeared forever. I remember going through the miniature-marshmallow phase of fish bait. It was disgusting. Pastel marshmallows! Remember? Arguments would break out over what was the best marshmallow bait, the pinks or the greenies. True anglers were ashamed to walk into a store and buy a package of pastel miniature marshmallows. "My little boy likes to eat them," you'd say to the clerk. "Yeah, sure," she'd say. "And my dog, Rex, plays the violin." Or maybe some other anglers would ask you what you caught your fish on, and you'd say a No. 16 Royal Coachman on a one-ounce tippet, and about then a miniature pink marshmallow would fall out of your fishing vest and bounce up and down on the dock like a Super Ball. And you would squish it with your foot, but it would be too late. What I hated most about bait marshmallows was that they wouldn't sink when they came off the hook. Soon there would be these rainbow waves of miniature marshmallow slopping around the lake. They were pretty, yes, but they lacked that gritty, smelly, slimy essence that true fishermen love about real fish bait.

Next came the canned-corn phase. Not just any canned corn would do either. It had to be white niblet corn. On opening day of fishing season, five thousand fishermen would descend on a little lake near my home, and every one of them would have his little can of white niblet corn. Some of the anglers would actually open the cans of corn at home on electric can openers! They were despised by the corn purists, who insisted on hacking open the can with a dull jackknife. Unlike marshmallows, the niblets of corn sank when they came off the hook. After the first couple weeks of fishing season, the bottom of the lake would be covered with fermenting corn. Toward the end of summer, the lake approached 85 proof. The perch were already pickled when you caught them. They would lie on their backs in the live well, hiccuping.

White niblet corn and miniature pastel marshmallows were enough to give an old-time wormer like myself the galloping shudders. Kids would go into a store and buy marshmallows and corn and think that was all there ever was to getting bait. When I was a boy, catching worms was more of a challenge than catching fish. Some of our worms were bigger than most of our fish. We bragged about big worms we had dug. We lied about bigger worms we hadn't dug. We were worm snobs. Artificial flies were for sissies. We'd ridicule a kid right off the creek for fishing a dry fly. "Whatsa matter," we'd say, "scared of worms?"

I was a good wormer, but not a great one. Dum-dum Harris was a great wormer—the best! If there had been an Olympic event for worming, Dum-dum would have taken the gold. He wasn't all that bright about most things. He'd been in fourth grade longer than most of us had been in school. The teacher thought of him almost as part of the woodwork. Once she tried to screw a pencil sharpener onto his chest. Dum-dum helped her! But he was a genius when it came to finding worms.

Toward the end of July, the clay soil in our part of the country would bake into one great ceramic tile. Once you had chipped through the tile, you would start shoveling your way toward China. It took you so long to dig down to moist earth, where a worm might possibly be, that by the time you discovered you'd dug a dry hole, it was too late to dig another. If you managed to find one worm, you could go fishing for a couple of hours, pinching little sections off him to rebait the hook. Finally, you would be down to one little half-inch section of worm, and you and your buddy would be fighting to see who got it. Then Dum-dum would show up. He would actually fish whole worms. If a worm got even a little soggy, he would toss it into the creek and bait up another one. Dum-dum was the first person I ever saw practice conspicuous consumption.

Finally, by August, the rest of the boys would be down to fishing with manure-pile worms, tiny, pale, squiggly things. Dum-dum would come along with a can overflowing with big fat night crawlers.

"Mighty sick-looking worms you got there," he'd say, flipping out a half-pound night crawler.

"Yeah," one of us would reply. "Well, you'd be sick-looking too, if you were raised in a manure pile."

Sometimes Dum-dum would take mercy on us. "C'mon, Dum-dum, give us some worms," we'd beg. "We dug up half the county and didn't find a single worm."

"Got just enough for myself," he'd say. "But I'll help you find some."

Then he'd turn around and look this way and that, studying various clods of dirt. After a bit, he would walk over to a clod and pull it up, revealing a whole convention of worms. Dum-dum, however, didn't perform this service free of charge. Usually it would cost us our school hot-lunch desserts until about next Easter. We could scarcely believe we had frittered away the easy worms of May and June and were now forced to pay loan-shark prices to Dum-dum.

One of the advantages of worming, we discovered early on, was that it discouraged little girls from wanting to go fishing with us. When we got to be sixteen, however, we learned that it also discouraged big girls from wanting to go fishing with us. Most of us switched to flies then, claiming that worms really weren't a sporting bait. After thirty years and more of fishing with flies and other artificial lures, few things would make me return to worms. One of them is a seven-pound bass that may have escaped Lonnie Bird up at Crawford Slough.

After the worm rancher had stacked up my little round paper cartons of fifty worms, I pulled out a couple dollar bills and asked him how much I owed him.

"Let's see," he said, scratching his head. "This is always the hard part. What's fifty cents times fifty? Shoot, I'll go get my calculator."

"Hey, don't bother," I said. "That works out to twenty-five dollars."

"It does? Okay, I'll take your word for it. That'll be twenty-five dollars."

"*Twenty-five dollars!*" I screamed. "That's fifty cents a worm!"

"Yep," he said, grinning. "Or you could pay me all your hot-lunch desserts up until next Easter."

"What?" I said. "Dum-dum? My gosh, it is you—Dum-dum Harris!"

I don't know why I hadn't recognized him right off. Not that many people go around with a pencil sharpener screwed to their chest.

Scoring

A couple of years ago, I was on an antelope hunt in Wyoming with William Harold (Hal) Nesbitt, the executive director of the Boone & Crockett Club. I tried to explain to Hal why some of my big game animals should have been listed in the Boone & Crockett record book, but he wouldn't listen. My one complaint about Boone & Crockett is that it's just too fussy about scoring. The McManus System of Big Game Trophy Scoring would simplify the whole business, and, of course, get me into the record book where I belong.

I told Hal about a great shot I had made on a huge elk in Montana a few years back. Even with the Boone & Crockett system, that elk would have scored 380 points.

"Well," Hal said, "you should have taken it to an official Boone & Crockett scorer."

"How could I do that?" I said. "I missed the elk. But only by an inch. So now you tell me I can't be in the Boone & Crockett because of one lousy inch! That's what I mean, Hal—you B&C guys are just too fussy."

If the people who run Boone & Crockett had any sensitivity at all to a hunter's feelings, they would include a category called "Near Misses on Big Game Trophies."

Another thing I told Hal was that Boone & Crockett should let the hunter score his own game and report it himself. Would I lie about the score? Of course not. It really irritates me that Boone & Crockett might assume I would be dishonest about such a serious matter.

Hal pointed out that in his excitement over his trophy the hunter might not follow the prescribed procedures for scoring and thereby arrive at a score not in agreement with the trophy's actual dimensions.

"Well, of course not," I said. "My scoring always exceeds the trophy's actual dimensions at the time of its demise. What we're talking about here is merely the process by which a game animal whose natural life span has been terminated at middle age or younger is allowed to reach full maturity in the hunter's mind, through a series of complicated calculations. Usually—nay, always—this maturing process results in massive racks of near-perfect symmetry. These become part of the hunter's permanent mental record of the animal. It's simply a matter of taking care to shoot an animal that possesses the right set of genes. If you wanted proof, we could send you a few chromosomes and you could study the antler genes in them and find that the genes coincide with our judgment of the trophy's dimensions at full maturity. Hey, how about that, Hal? Good idea?"

That's a problem with the executive director of the Boone & Crockett Club. He doesn't know a really good idea when he hears one. Still, I thought when he returned to his office in Washington, D.C., Nesbitt would at least ponder my suggestions and eventually come to realize the good sense they make. But no. I have just received a book titled *Measuring and Scoring North American Big Game Trophies* by none other than William H. Nesbitt and a coauthor, Dr. Philip L. Wright. Not once is the McManus Trophy Scoring System mentioned, and I had to read the whole darn book to find that out.

Until I manage to bring out *The Complete McManus Book of Scoring Big Game Trophies* (three pages, with large illustrations), hunters who want to see how their big game ranks according to Boone & Crockett standards may want to get a copy of the Nesbitt-Wright book.

The book includes all score charts and procedures and "covers all thirty-four categories of native big game." I must admit I was surprised by the thirty-four categories of big game. I thought there were only bear, deer, elk, goat, antelope, sheep, moose, and turkey. Strangely, Nesbitt and Wright overlooked turkey, but include walrus and muskox! I suppose walrus and muskox are all right, but I think the authors made a monumental error in omitting turkey. They are no doubt prejudiced by the fact that the turkey has only two legs, unless you count the turkey my wife bought for last Thanksgiving, which had three. Well, I told her I wasn't going to eat any deformed, mutated turkey no matter how much she threatened me, but it tasted all right. Now where was I? Oh, yes, the walrus doesn't have any legs at all to speak of, and Nesbitt and Wright included it. So why not put in the turkey? Just ask yourself, which would your spouse let you display in the living room, a mount of a walrus or a turkey? Right, neither one, but just for the sake of argument, ask yourself that.

Even though *Measuring and Scoring North American Big Game Trophies* fails to include the McManus System or turkey, I found myself studying and memorizing pertinent information in some of the chapters and charts.

I figured that the next time I went to a big game show, I could use it. I'd walk up to a guy standing smugly next to his monstrous elk rack and say, "Note the point developed from the side of the main beam adjacent to the normal point, G-4. Do you understand what I mean by G-4? Why, it's this point right here. On a Roosevelt's elk, this point would be considered normal and designated as G-5. On an American elk, as you have here, it is considered abnormal. Too bad, pal. You must take your horns and leave immediately."

One of the best sections in the book is instructions on how to calculate the score of your own trophy, using common tools found around the house: calipers, carpenter square, alligator clips, tape measure, and so on. I've already had occasion to use my information. At Kelly's Bar and Grill the other night, I happened to hear a couple of young bachelor friends of mine, Phil and Ernie, mention the word "scoring." From the intensity of their discussion, I judged they were very serious about the subject, and Phil indicated it was a matter of prime importance for him to score that very evening. Why he would put off scoring a trophy until after dark I didn't know, but Phil, as you will see, is a bit odd anyway.

"Hey, scoring," I said, "I'm something of an expert on that."

They both laughed. "C'mon, man, quit putting us on," Phil said presently. "A pudgy old guy like you? Ha!"

"Oh yeah?" I said. "I'll have you know I just finished reading a book about it. I bet you guys don't even know the basic equipment for scoring."

I could tell I had them there, because they both looked embarrassed.

" 'Ha!' yourself," I said. "I thought so. Sure, you probably figure all you need is a carpenter's square and a measuring tape. But I'll bet you've never even considered using a caliper."

"Get away, man!" Phil said. "I don't want to hear it!"

"I thought not," I said. "And how about alligator clips? You've never even considered them, have you?"

"Hey, c'mon!" Phil said, grimacing. "You're getting too weird even for ole Ernie here."

"You guys just don't want to learn how to do a thing right," I said. "You probably won't even bother to read my book, *The McManus System of Scoring*, when it comes out."

"Probably not," Ernie said.

"In any case, you should learn proper scoring technique," I said. "For example, Ernie, that moose I saw you with last fall could have made Boone & Crockett."

Well, I don't know what set Ernie off, but he went bonkers. I suppose he'd been drinking too much coffee or not getting enough sleep. Anyway, while Phil wrestled him to the floor, I made a quick exit, recalling belatedly that some people just can't take a compliment, and Ernie is one of them.

Later, I learned that there might have been some confusion in the use of the word "scoring" between the boys and me. Apparently, in some quarters "scoring" means successfully making the acquaintance of a person of the opposite sex and questionable character. I was a little embarrassed by the misunderstanding, I'll admit, but nevertheless I had managed to save both Phil and Ernie from achieving their unsavory purpose: Kelly's bartender chucked the two of them into the street because of the ruckus. They'll thank me someday, too, although from what I hear from mutual friends, it won't be anytime in the near future.

A Road Less Traveled By

In his poem "The Road Not Taken," Robert
Frost wrote of two roads diverging in a wood, and
he took "the one less traveled by." It's a wonder he didn't
see me somewhere along the way. I was wearing my
cowboy hat, a red-and-black plaid shirt, and a worried
look. People who take roads less traveled by often wear
worried looks.

I love driving roads less traveled by, the lesser the
better. My wife, Bun, and I were huckleberrying in the
mountains the other day, and I pointed to a road less
traveled by that diverged off the main Forest Service
arterial. "Let's go up that road," I said. "Probably find
some good picking."

"What road?" she said. "I don't see any road."

"Right there," I said. "On the other side of the ditch.
The tracks are grown over a bit with brush, but you can
see where the road starts to wind up the mountain.
Brush in the track is a good sign, because that indicates
no one has gone up the road in a while. Therefore, we

can conclude that no one has picked the berries on top of the mountain."

"Brush? *Trees* are growing in that track!"

"Well, yes, but they are small trees. That's even better, because it tells us that no one has gone up the road in a couple of years."

"Or possibly this century!" Bun cried. "We're not going up that 'road,' as you so imaginatively describe it. That's nothing but a crack in the woods!"

"And you claim to be a devotee of Robert Frost," I said. "What would old Bob think of you now?"

"Frost? What's he got to do with this insanity?"

"Never mind. Anyway, what we'll do is just drive up the road a little ways, and if it looks too rough, we'll turn around and come back."

Reluctantly, Bun accepted this suggestion, which is an old but good ruse, and wives usually fall for it.

I put the spurs to Hoss, my old four-wheel-drive, and we went bucking and snorting through the ditch and up the bank to the road less traveled by, scarcely bouncing enough to flatten the crown of my cowboy hat against the roof of the cab. Bun slid her glasses back up her nose and checked the buckle on her seat belt. "I really hate this," she joked. I laughed appreciatively at her spunky wit.

Hoss plowed through the ten-foot-high brush, plodded on through a small rocky stream, and almost pooped out in a swampy area on the far side. Then he charged up to high ground, where the road, or possibly an old avalanche, was strewn with boulders the size of basketballs. We maneuvered around some of the basketballs, climbed over the rest, and sent a few of them dribbling down the grade behind us. A pile of shale had slid off the mountain onto the road ahead of us. One side of

Hoss was wedged up against a rock wall; the other side extended out over a precipice by half the width of a tire.

"Stop!" Bun demanded shrilly. "Turn around and go back this instant!"

Calmly discharging cold sweat, I ignored her absurd demand. To distract her from the illusion that we were in an impossible predicament, I exclaimed cheerily, "Look, Bun, a bald eagle! Don't you love to watch eagles soar?"

"Not when I'm looking straight down at them," she said.

"Yes," I said, "this perspective does take something away from their majesty. Well, I'm sure the road will improve soon."

I was lying, of course. Roads less traveled by never get better, only worse. Still, a modest white lie does little harm and some good. It can calm a nervous spouse and distract her from clawing up the upholstery.

"Now," I said, "when we go over that shale pile ahead, we will tilt rather sharply toward the brink of the cliff and may even slide sideways a few inches, but that is only normal in situations such as this."

I could see that these words had the desired calming effect on Bun, because she dabbed the perspiration from her forehead with a swatch of upholstery and even gave me a tiny, if grim, smile. Smiling with clenched teeth produces a rather grotesque effect, however, and I made a mental note to call this to her attention at a later time, provided there was a later time.

We crossed the shale pile without harm, except for possible hearing loss as the result of loud shrieking in a closed cab. As I told Bun, loud shrieking is wonderful for relieving tension and she should have joined in. I get really annoyed at people who bottle up their tension.

As I expected, the road deteriorated quickly beyond the shale pile, and old Hoss began to whinny and slip and stumble. "Well," I said, "time to drop into four-wheel drive. I know some outdoorsmen who are so stupid they drive into a remote place in four-wheel drive until they get stuck. Then they're up the creek. The thing to do is go in two-wheel until you get stuck and then you have four-wheel to get you out."

"Guess what," Bun said. "You put it in four-wheel crossing the swamp and never took it out."

"Quite correct," I said. "I was just checking to see if you remembered. You see, I had an ace up my sleeve all along. The power winch! Now, if you would be so kind as to pull out the winch cable and attach it to the trunk of one of those trees protruding from the avalanche, we will be on our way again. I would do it myself but I don't want to take the time to pry my fingers off the steering wheel."

Winching the last few hundred yards to the top of the mountain was slow and tedious, with Bun slogging ahead to hook the cable. I thought I should probably install a faster winch—or a faster wench! Ha! Wisdom being the better part of valor, I kept that little joke to myself, Bun seeming oddly out of sorts at the time.

Suddenly, I noticed Bun wildly waving her arms and shouting at me. Thinking this might be a warning the cable was about to snap and send me and Hoss hurtling off the mountain, I sprang sprightly from the cab and drained off the spurt of excessive adrenaline by hopping smartly in place. "What?" I shouted. "What is it?"

"Huckleberries!" Bun shouted. "Tons of them! And they're as big as cherries! Bring the buckets!"

"Huckleberries?" I said. "What do you want with huckleberries?"

I hate picking huckleberries. I don't care if they're as big as grapefruit. What did Bun think, that I'd come all this way on a less-traveled road to pick huckleberries?

"I said," Bun shouted sternly, *"bring the buckets!* And you know what's even better? There are huckleberry pickers!"

"There can't be huckleberry pickers," I said. "Not on a road less traveled by."

"Yeah, there are," Bun said. "I-90 cuts across the mountain here. Isn't that great? We don't have to go back down that awful road."

I don't know where Robert Frost ended up on his road less traveled by, but I doubt it was a four-lane interstate. I've been depressed ever since.

Gunkholing

One of the problems with gunkholing is that many boaters don't know what it is. I have just taken a scientific survey of four boaters, and none of them knew the meaning of the word *gunkholing*. (They did make several guesses, all of which were wrong and pretty weird to boot. It's a good thing for them that I'm not a Freudian psychologist or they would be in a lot of trouble right now.) Even my unabridged *Random House Dictionary of the English Language* contains *gunk hole*, which it defines as "a quiet anchorage, as in a cove." It defines *gunkholing* as "to sail casually along a coast, anchoring from time to time in quiet coves and inlets." If a simple lexicographer knows the meaning of *gunkholing*, you would certainly expect boaters to, since they're the ones who do it.

All right, I'll confess. I was past puberty before I knew a gunk hole from a gopher hole. About twenty years past puberty, but so what? I didn't bring the subject up.

An editor did. He wrote me a letter requesting that I write an article on gunkholing.

"I'm sure you know what it means," he wrote evasively, "but don't bother looking in your Webster's dictionary because it isn't in there."

Well, of course, it wouldn't be in *that* dictionary. Webster wasn't the sort of man who would know about gunkholing and wouldn't admit it if he did.

Now that I've taken care of the definition of *gunkholing*, I had better tell you how it's done properly. There's a lot of slipshod gunkholing going on among boaters nowadays, which is probably another one of those signs of the times we're always hearing about. People just don't want to take the time to learn how to do a thing properly, the way God intended. Do I think God approves of gunkholing? Why, of course I do. He approves of all the good things, and gunkholing is one of the good things. When you stop and think about it, the Garden of Eden was sort of one great big gunk hole, with Adam and Eve laid back, taking it easy, and not a worry in the garden. Then Eve got hungry. What ruins a lot of fine gunkholing is somebody's getting hungry. That's when all the trouble usually starts. Let me give you one example.

My friend Retch Sweeney and I were fishing up on Lake Roosevelt one day a couple of summers ago, and all the fish had fallen into a comatose state and sunk to the bottom as they like to do when I'm in the vicinity. Then a rare and startling thing happened. Retch got an idea.

"Hey, I got an idea!" he said, appearing no less amazed than myself. "Let's find us a nice gunk hole and tie up to a tree for the rest of the afternoon. We can lay back and take it easy until the evening feed."

I knew we weren't properly prepared for serious gunkholing, but since this was Retch's first idea in several months it seemed a shame to waste it.

"That's a good idea," I said. "Let's do it."

It took us nearly an hour to find a halfway decent gunk hole, one with some shade on the water and an aesthetically pleasing backdrop of trees and moss-covered rocks, and a tiny stream tumbling melodiously down a picturesque precipice. There was one drawback. A hundred yards above us, a highway wound around the mountain, and the roar of traffic drifted down to our otherwise peaceful gunk hole. Worse yet, there was a roadhouse up there, and we could hear the banging of the screen door, the raucous voices of the clientele coming and going, and occasionally even the sound of glasses and plates knocking together.

"Kind of noisy for proper gunkholing," I said.

"Yeah," Retch said. "Just have to ignore it, I guess."

We spread out the boat cushions and lay down on them. The boat rocked gently in the waves, a bird twittered, the water made appropriate water sounds against the shore. Presently, Retch said, "This is nice, ain't it?"

"Yes," I said. "A man needs gunkholing from time to time, you know what I mean?"

"Yeah."

Then Retch said from beneath the hat over his face, "They're cooking hamburgers up in that roadhouse. I can smell 'em."

"You're probably just smelling that hat."

"No, it's hamburgers. Big, fat, juicy hamburgers."

A period of silence.

"We got anything left to eat in the lunchbox?" Retch asked.

"Just half a peanut butter and jelly sandwich."

"Ugh."

A period of silence.

Retch suddenly sat up. "They got thick slabs of sweet onion on those big fat juicy hamburgers. Now, don't tell me you can't smell that onion."

"No, I don't. That roadhouse is a hundred yards away, up on top of that cliff. You're just imagining you're smelling big fat juicy hamburgers with thick slabs of sweet onion on them. Now are we going to gunkhole or not?"

Retch lurched to his feet and stared at the cliff. "Probably wouldn't take more than ten minutes to climb up to that roadhouse."

"Are you crazy, man?" I said. "A person could kill himself trying to climb that cliff!"

Retch's nose twitched, as if savoring the aroma of a big fat juicy hamburger with a thick slab of sweet onion on it. "I got to try!" he croaked, stepping out of the boat and heading for the roadhouse. Unfortunately, the boat was in fifteen feet of water. He shot out of sight in a giant splash, only to emerge a minute later scrambling over the moss-covered rocks like a frightened crab. He slipped on the wet moss and fell into the melodious stream, cursing both roundly. Scarcely had I recovered from a fit of mirth over this spectacle when I saw his hulking figure clawing its way up the side of the cliff. Retch hung by one hand from a tiny bump in the cliff while his legs churned against the rock in search of a foothold. A short while later he seemed to be clamped to the granite wall with nothing but his fingernails. What worried me was that he hadn't got to the bad part of the cliff yet.

Eventually, he threw a leg up over the lip of the cliff

and vanished. I heaved a sigh of disgust and flopped back down on boat cushions, trying to recapture some of the passive enjoyment of gunkholing. Scarcely had I closed my eyes, however, when I heard a little shower of rocks rattling down the cliff. I glanced up, and there was Retch again, clawing his way back down. Twenty minutes later he was back at the boat.

"You . . . *pant* . . . ought to see those . . . *gasp* . . . hamburgers! They are . . . *choke* . . . magnificent!"

"So why aren't you up there eating one of them?" I asked.

"I . . . *gasp* . . . forgot my billfold. It's . . . *pant* . . . in my tackle box. Get it for me . . . *choke* . . . will you?"

I tossed him his billfold, and he staggered off again in the direction of the cliff. His ascent this time was so horrifying and verbally obscene that I will not describe it, in case this is being read by children.

Two hours later, while I was napping peacefully in the boat, I was suddenly attacked by a tattered, wild-eyed creature that came lurching out of the brush on shore. Snatching up an oar, I attempted to repel the beast, only to discover at the last moment that it was Retch Sweeney himself, or at least what was left of him. I hauled him into the boat.

"I've had enough gunkholing," I told him. "The fish have regained consciousness and are starting to feed. Now that we've had a good rest, we should be able to get in a couple of hours of hard fishing before dark."

"Mmmffff," Retch replied, in a tone that suggested a definite lack of enthusiasm.

I tried to cheer him up. "Nothing like a little restful gunkholing to get the old juices flowing!"

"Phimmph," he said, rather crossly.

"Well," I went on cheerily, "how was the big fat juicy hamburger? Can you honestly say that it was worth all the risk and effort and trouble?"

"Yeah, it was."

"Really?"

"Best burger I ever ate. It was charbroiled, but juicy pink on the inside. The buns were homemade and toasted on the grill. Then they were slathered with this special sauce. Next, thick slices of tomato and cheese were loaded on."

"Tomato, too?"

"Yeah. And nice fresh crisp lettuce. Next came this big slab of Walla Walla sweet onion. Oh, it was enough to drive a hungry gunkholer out of his mind."

"Good onion, hunh?"

"Delicious! Scrumptious! Then they heaped on the side this huge pile of steaming hot, thick, crunchy-on-the-outside, soft-on-the-inside french fries. Oh, man, let me tell you, was that ever a good burger!"

"Well, Retch," I said, shaking my head, "after you risked life and limb climbing that cliff for a hamburger, let me ask you this."

"What?"

"When you reach that overhang at the top of the cliff, do you think it's easier to throw your right leg over it first or your left?"

That is a classic example of improper gunkholing. Here, now, are the rules for proper gunkholing.

1. Take plenty of food and beverage, since gunkholing stimulates a ravenous appetite. A good supply of edibles will usually discourage members of the party from going

ashore to forage at roadhouses, farmhouses, and camp-
ground garbage cans.

2. If your spouse is along, do not allow her to persuade
you to disembark for the purpose of picking up a nice
piece of driftwood, collecting a strange weed, or obtain-
ing an unusual rock for the rock garden at home. My
wife once talked me into going out into a waterfront
cow pasture to commit theft on a rock shaped vaguely
like a washbasin. Although it was shaped like a washbasin, it weighed approximately the same as a bathtub,
filled, and with a fat lady in it. No sooner had I wrenched
the rock loose from the earth in which it had been
embedded by the last glacier to pass through than the
herd of cows resident in the pasture raised a cry of alarm
and took off after me in a frenzy to thwart the burglary.
I sprinted for the safety of the boat, all the while mindful
of how ridiculous it appears for a man to sprint with his
legs bowed out in the configuration of a barrel hoop
and his arms stretched practically to the ground from
the weight of a monstrous boulder. Naturally, my wife
started screaming. "Don't drop the rock!" she screamed.
"Don't drop the rock!"

Never be persuaded to go ashore while gunkholing.

3. Gunkhole only with persons who don't tell jokes.
Nothing ruins gunkholing faster than a compulsive joke-
teller. You will be pulling into a peaceful cove where
the foliage of the shoreline is mirrored in the water, the
stillness of the place is broken only by the distant call of
a loon, a doe and her fawn are slipping out of the shadows for a drink, the hillside above is golden in the sun-
light and sprinkled with wildflowers. Then your
companion will blurt out, "Say, did I ever tell you the
one about the farmer's daughter and the Russian cos-
monaut? Well, it seems . . . "

There is one sure cure for the compulsive joke-teller while gunkholing, but I can tell you only that it involves an anchor and a length of rope.

4. Don't gunkhole at night with an attractive person of the opposite sex, particularly when golden moonbeams dance on undulating waves, a gentle breeze whispers sweet nothings to the stars, and mingled fragrances of pine and cedar caress each breath of air, unless of course you have a serious relationship with the person, and then it's okay.

There are many other rules to proper gunkholing, but I don't have time to go into them now. Even as I write this I am bobbing about in one of the finest gunk holes I have ever discovered. Its only fault is a rather noisy drive-in restaurant on the highway up above. If I have not mistaken the aroma, the specialty of the house is char-grilled hot dogs smothered in relish and heaped with chopped onions. Many persons might think the terrain between me and the drive-in totally untraversable, but what do they know about gunkholing?

Blips

I seem to spend a good part of my life pushing buttons. If I want to cook a pizza, I stick it in
a microwave oven, push a few buttons, and presto, I
have melted cheese all over the oven. I push buttons to
set the temperature of the house and car, to turn on
radios, TVs, and VCRs, to type, to set my watch and
clocks and the speed of my car, and even to get cash
out of my bank, in the rare instance when there is cash
there to get.

Buttons, as anglers well know, now play a big role in
fishing, particularly as they apply to fish-finders. Much
fishing nowadays consists of pushing buttons while staring at blips on a screen.

"Wow, look at that one!" the modern angler exclaims,
staring at a blip. "It's dang near an inch long. I bet that
blip would go five pounds!"

Many anglers now consider a day's fishing successful
if they've seen a few large blips. Soon, anglers will start
mounting their biggest blips and hanging them on den

walls. "I tied into that blip up on Lake Weegee," the angler will brag. "Biggest blip ever recorded at Weegee."

I've already noticed a tendency among my friends to exaggerate the size of their blips. I suspect a good deal of lying goes on about monstrous blips that got away.

As my friend Keith Jackson likes to say, though, you can't eat blips. (It's not that good of a saying, but it's the best Jackson has come up with, so he says it over and over.) He means that sooner or later you have to bait a hook and dangle it down in front of whatever is causing the blip. Blip purists, of course, consider actual fishing to be bad form, crude and distasteful.

Jackson always has the latest in electronic fish-finders, because he does a lot of writing about high-tech fishing. After many years of scientific experimentation, he has worked out a simple and efficient method for dealing with faulty technology in fishing gear. He sells it to me.

As we were visiting in his fishing-tackle warehouse—formerly his garage—he said to me recently, "Hey, I got a new fish-finder for you."

"What's wrong with it?"

"Nothing. It's the most advanced fish-finder I've ever come across."

"I'll bet! How much you want for it?"

"Well, you being a good buddy and all, I'm going to let you have it for noth . . . noth . . . for twenty-five dollars."

"Twenty-five dollars! Let me see this worthless piece of junk."

Jackson pointed to a nice wooden box, the lid of which had been nailed shut, with most of the nails bent over and surrounded by the indentations of a wildly flailed hammer.

"So, let me have a look at the thing," I said.

"I'd prefer you take it home and look at it there." He seemed nervous.

"No doubt," I said.

Reluctantly, Jackson pried up the lid on the box. I looked in. The little high-tech face of the fish-finder stared back at me.

"Looks like new," I said.

"It is new," Jackson said. "I only used it once."

"Conked out on you, hunh?"

"Nope, worked fine."

"Well, the price is right," I said.

"Yep," Jackson said. *"Heh heh heh."*

A few days later, I hooked up the fish-finder to my boat and went out on the lake to see if I could turn up a few blips for supper. After pushing a few buttons on the control panel of the finder without results, I resorted to an old trick I learned years ago: reading the operation manual.

The manual informed me that my finder had been given its own individual name—Melvin. It said that not only did Melvin accurately report water depth, temperature, and pH and location, size, and species of fish, it also offered advice on the kind of lure to use and how to fish it. "Your Melvin 500X contains a small but powerful computer into which has been fed all the fishing knowledge, lore, expertise, and wisdom of an actual eighty-year-old angler. The Melvin 500X also captures much of the crusty old angler's personality, which we at FISHTECH are sure you will find amusing and entertaining. You and Melvin enjoy your fishin' now, hear?"

"Holy cow!" I said to myself. "I can't believe Jackson sold me this fantastic piece of technology for only twenty-five dollars. He must have been out of his mind."

As instructed by the manual, I punched in the secret

code to activate the fish-finder. *Beep beep beep* went the little black box, followed by: "Howdy, bub. Name's Melvin. How you today? Well, we can't catch no fish sittin' here chewin' the fat. Crank up the motor and take us out to a depth of twenty feet. Don't just sit there with you thumb in you mouth. Git crackin'!"

Hey, this is terrific, I thought. It's almost like having the old angler right here in the boat with me. I watched the depth scale on the finder screen blink toward twenty feet.

"Why so quiet, bub?" the finder asked. "Cat got your tongue?"

"What?" I said, startled. "You mean you can hear me?"

"Sure I can hear you. Just because I'm an ugly little black box don't mean I'm deaf. Jeez cripes, look out for that log! You got to pay attention, bub. I hope you fish better than you drive a boat."

"Sorry, uh, Melvin," I said. "I was a little distracted there for a moment." I felt a little silly, apologizing to an ugly little black box.

The depth scale read twenty feet, but there were no blips on the screen. Because I was after largemouth bass blips, I decided to run on up to another spot I knew.

"What you think you doin'?" Melvin said. "We're gonna fish here."

"But there aren't any fish here," I said. "There's not a single blip on the screen."

"Don't pay no attention to that stupid screen, bub. It don't know nothin'. If I say there's bass here, there's bass here. I can feel it in my bones . . . well, in my transistors, anyway. There's bass down there all right, huggin' the bottom. Go about five pounds. Tie on a whitehead jig baited with a purple worm. Bounce it along the bottom."

"I think a chartreuse worm would work better," I said.

"You sassin' me, boy? I say purple worm, I mean purple worm!"

I tied on a purple worm and began bouncing it along the bottom. Nothing. Melvin was beginning to get on my nerves. For one thing, he kept humming tunelessly. Presently, he said, "Knock knock."

"What?" I said.

"Not 'what,' dummy," Melvin snapped. "You supposed to say 'Who's there?' "

"Stop!" I shouted. "I hate knock-knock jokes."

"Tough," Melvin said. "I'm supposed to entertain you, and this is the entertainment. Now I ain't gonna tell you again. Knock knock."

Just then I hooked into something and started to reel in.

"Five-pound largemouth," Melvin said.

"I don't think so," I said.

"If I say it's a five-pound largemouth, it's a five-pound largemouth."

I hauled a waterlogged branch into the boat. "Ha!" I said, holding up the branch. "What do you say this is, Melvin?"

"I say it's a five-pound largemouth," Melvin said.

"I've had about enough out of you, Melvin," I snarled.

"You sass me again, boy, I gonna whomp your head!"

"Okay, that's it. I'm going to jerk your power cord," a threat I instantly carried out. The screen went dark. I was left with peace and quiet, a huge expanse of sparkling water, and only my own wild guesses to tell me where the fish might be.

"Knock knock," the black box said.

"Melvin?" I said. "But I pulled your plug."

"Ever hear of batteries, bub? I come with a backup power supply. Now, one more time—knock knock."

I snatched up the black box. "That was your last knock knock. I'm going to deep-six you!"

"Help! Help!" the black box squawked. "Murder! Help!"

Melvin landed with a splash and sank. Then he bobbed back to the surface. The FISHTECH engineers had had the malicious foresight to equip the black box with flotation. Little paddles popped out of Melvin's sides and he started to churn his way back to the boat, cursing a blue streak all the while. I pushed him off with an oar, started the motor, and headed for home, glancing back from time to time to see if I was being followed. Sure enough . . .

Suddenly, I awoke in a cold sweat. It was the middle of the night. I was safe in my own bed.

"For heaven's sake, what is it?" my wife, Bun, asked.

"Nothing," I said. "I just thought I heard something go 'knock knock.' "

"You did," Bun said. "It's at the front door. Who could it be at this hour?"

"I think I know," I said. "Don't answer it."

The Night the Bear
Ate Goombaw

There was so much confusion over the incident anyway that I don't want to add to it by getting the sequences mixed up. First of all—and I remember this clearly—it was the summer after Crazy Eddie Muldoon and I had been sprung from third grade at Delmore Blight Grade School. The Muldoons' only good milk cow died that summer, shortly after the weasel got in their chicken house and killed most of the laying hens. This was just before the fertilizer company Mr. Muldoon worked for went bankrupt, and he lost his job. The engine on his tractor blew up a week later, so he couldn't harvest his crops, which were all pretty much dried up from the drought anyway.

Then Mr. Muldoon fell in the pit trap that Crazy Eddie and I had dug to capture wild animals. Our plan was to train the wild animals and then put on shows to earn a little extra money for the family. But Mr. Muldoon fell in the trap, and afterwards made us shovel all the dirt back into it. The only wild animal we had trapped was a skunk, and when Mr. Muldoon fell in on top of it, he terrified the poor creature practically to death. Neither Mr. Muldoon nor the skunk was hurt much, but the skunk managed to escape during all the excitement. So there went our wild-animal show. This occurred about midsummer, as I recall, about the time Mr. Muldoon's nerves got so bad that old Doc Hix told him to stop drinking coffee, which apparently was what had brought on his nervous condition.

For the rest of the summer, Mr. Muldoon gave off a faint, gradually fading odor of skunk. Unless he got wet. Then the odor reconstituted itself to approximately its original power, which placed a major restraint on the Muldoons' social life, meager as that was. Fortunately, Mr. Muldoon didn't get wet that often, mainly because of the drought that had killed off his crops. As Mrs. Muldoon was fond of saying, every cloud has a silver lining.

So far it had been a fairly typical summer for Mr. Muldoon, but he claimed to be worried about a premonition that his luck was about to turn bad. Then Eddie's grandmother, Mrs. Muldoon's mother, showed up for a visit.

"I knew it!" Mr. Muldoon told a neighbor. "I knew something like this was about to happen! I must be physic."

After I got to know Eddie's grandmother a little better, I could see why Mr. Muldoon regarded her visit as a stroke of bad luck. She immediately assumed command of the family and began to boss everyone around, including me. Nevertheless, I doubted that Mr. Muldoon was actually physic, because otherwise he would never have come up with the idea of the camping trip.

"I'm worried about Pa," Eddie said one morning as

we sat on his back porch. "He's not been hisself lately."

"Who's he been?" I asked, somewhat startled, although I regarded Mr. Muldoon as one of the oddest persons I knew.

"Pa's just started acting weird, that's all. You know what crazy idea he came up with this morning? He says we all gotta go on a camping trip up in the mountains and pick huckleberries. He says we can sell any extra huckleberries we get for cash. But Pa don't know anything about camping. We don't even have any camping stuff. Ain't that strange?"

"Yeah," I said. "Say, Eddie, you don't suppose your pa . . . uh . . . your pa . . ." I tried to think of a delicate way to phrase it.

"What?" Eddie said.

"Uh, you don't suppose your pa, uh, would let me go on the camping trip too, do you?"

When Eddie put the question to his father, Mr. Muldoon tried to conceal his affection for me beneath a malevolent frown. "Oh, all right," he growled at me. "But no mischief. That means no knives, no hatchets, no matches, no slingshots, and *no shovels!* Understood?"

Eddie and I laughed. It was good to see his father in a humorous mood once again.

I rushed home and asked my mother if I could go camping with the Muldoons. "You'd be away from home a whole week?" she said. "I'll have to think about that. Okay, you can go."

I quickly packed my hatchet, knife, and slingshot, along with edibles Mom gave me to contribute to the Muldoon grub box. The one major item I lacked was a sleeping bag. "I'll just make a bedroll out of some blankets off my bed," I informed my mother.

"You most certainly won't," she informed me. "You'll use the coat."

"Ah, gee, Ma, the coat's so stupid. Mr. Muldoon will tease me all during the trip if I have to use that stupid coat for a sleeping bag."

The coat in question was a tattered, dog-chewed old fur of indeterminate species that my grandmother had acquired during a brief period of family wealth in the previous century. It had been given to me as a "sleeping bag" for my frequent but always aborted attempts at sleeping out alone in the yard. For all its hideous appearance, it was warm and cozy, and covered my nine-year-old body nicely from end to end. Still, I knew the Muldoons would laugh themselves silly when they saw me bed down in a woman's fur coat. My only hope of retaining a shred of dignity, not to mention my carefully nursed macho image, was to slip into it after they had all gone to sleep. I stuffed the coat into a gunnysack, concealing it under the one threadbare blanket my mother reluctantly issued me.

The day of the big camping trip dawned bright and clear, a common ruse of Mother Nature to lure unsuspecting souls out into the wilds. The five of us piled into the ancient Muldoon sedan and set off for the mountains. Most of our camping gear, such as it was, balanced precariously atop the car. It was wrapped in a huge hay tarp, which was to serve as our tent. "Ain't had a drop of rain in three months," Mr. Muldoon had said. "Probably won't need the tarp." This statement would later be recalled and admitted as evidence in the case against Mr. Muldoon's being physic.

"How you doin' back there, Goombaw?" Mr. Muldoon said to Eddie's grandmother. For some reason, everyone called her Goombaw.

"How you think I'm doin'?" Goombaw snapped back. "Wedged in between these two sweaty younguns! I'm boilin' in my own juice! This camping trip is the stupidest dang fool idear you ever come up with, Herbert! We'll probably all get et by bears. Tell me, what about bears, Herbert?"

Yeah, I thought. What about bears?

"Ha ha ha ha," Mr. Muldoon laughed. "You don't have to worry about bears. They're more afraid of humans than we are of them."

Well, I thought, that's certainly not true of all humans, particularly one that I know personally. It's probably not true of all bears either. But I kept these thoughts to myself, since Goombaw was doing a thorough job of grilling Mr. Muldoon on the subject. I could tell that the talk of bears was making Mrs. Muldoon nervous, not that she was the only one.

"Let's change the subject, Goombaw," she said.

"Oh, all right. How about mountain lions, Herbert?"

For the rest of the long, hot, dusty ride up to the huckleberry patches, Goombaw harangued Mr. Muldoon about every possible threat to our well-being, from bears to crazed woodcutters. By the time we reached our campsite, she had everyone in such a nervous state that we were almost afraid to get out of the car. Mr. Muldoon stepped out, swiveled his head about as though expecting an attack from any quarter, and then ordered us to help set up camp.

No level area for our tent was immediately apparent, but Crazy Eddie and I finally located one. It was down a steep bank and on the far side of a little creek. Mr. Muldoon, Eddie, and I dragged the bundle of camp gear down the bank and across a log to the little clearing in the brush and trees. In no time at all Mr. Muldoon had constructed a fine shelter out of the tarp. Eddie and I built a fire ring of rocks, and Mrs. Muldoon and Goombaw got a fire going and put coffee on to boil, apparently forgetting that the doctor had told Mr. Muldoon to cut down on his coffee drinking because of his nerves. Eddie and I sampled the fishing in the creek. All in all, the camping trip showed signs of becoming a pleasant experience. Then it got dark.

"I say keep a fire goin' all night," Goombaw advised. "It might help keep the bears off of us."

"There ain't no bears," Mr. Muldoon said. "Now stop worrying about bears. Ha! Bears are more afraid of us than we are of them. Now, everybody get a good night's sleep. We got a lot of huckleberries to pick tomorrow." He stripped down to his long underwear and burrowed into the pile of quilts and blankets Mrs. Muldoon had arranged on the ground.

I pulled my threadbare blanket out of the gunnysack and spread it out in the dirt next to Goombaw.

"Good heavens, Patrick!" Mrs. Muldoon said. "Is that all you have to sleep in, that one little blanket? The nights can get pretty chilly up here in the mountains."

"Oh, I've got more blankets in my sack," I lied. "If it turns cold, I'll just put some more on. But I sleep warm."

As the night dragged on into its full depth, I lay there shivering in my blanket, studying with considerable interest the looming dark shapes the full moon revealed around our camp. Finally, Goombaw and the Muldoons ceased their thrashing about on the hard ground and began to emit the sounds of sleep. I jerked the fur coat out of the gunnysack and buttoned myself into its comforting warmth. I set a mental alarm to awaken me before the Muldoons, so I could conceal the coat before they caught sight of the hideous thing. Then I drifted off into fitful sleep.

"Wazzat?" Goombaw shouted in my ear.

Later, she claimed only to be having a nightmare, but, fortunately for us, she sounded the alarm just in time. In the silence that followed Goombaw's shout, you could almost hear four pairs of eyelids popping open in the dark.

"A bear!" Goombaw shouted. "A bear's got me!"

Since I was lying right next to Goombaw, this announcement aroused my curiosity no end. I tried to leap to my feet but, wrapped in the fur coat, could only manage to make it to all fours.

"Bear!" screamed Crazy Eddie. "Bear's got Gooooo—!"

"Bear!" shrieked Mrs. Muldoon. "There it is!"

Goombaw made a horrible sound. I could make out the big round whites of her eyes fixed on me in the darkness, no doubt pleading wordlessly with me for help, but what could a small boy do against a bear?

"Holy bleep!" roared Mr. Muldoon. He lunged to his feet, knocking over the ridgepole and dropping the tarp on us and the bear. Figuring Goombaw already for a goner and myself next on the bear's menu, I tore out from under the tarp just in time to see Mr. Muldoon trying to unstick an ax from the stump in which he had embedded it the night before. Even in the shadowy dimness of moonlight, I could see the look of surprise and horror wash over Mr. Muldoon's face as I rushed toward him for protection. He emitted a strangled cry and rushed off through the woods on legs so wobbly it looked as if his knees had come unhinged. Under the circumstances, I could only surmise that the bear was close on my heels, and I raced off after Mr. Muldoon, unable to think of anything better to do. With his abrupt departure, Mr. Muldoon had clearly let it be known that now it was every man for himself.

Bounding over a log with the effortless ease that accompanies total panic, I came upon Mr. Muldoon peeling bark and limbs off a small tree. Since he was only four feet up the tree, I debated briefly whether to wait for him to gain altitude or to find my own tree. Then Mr. Muldoon caught sight of the bear closing fast on us. He sprang out of the tree and took off again, with me so close behind that I could have reached out and grabbed the snapping flap of his long underwear. The thought did occur to me to do so, because I was nearing exhaustion, and Mr. Muldoon could have towed me along with his underwear flap. Upon later reflection, however, I think it is well that I didn't grab the flap, for it probably would have been a source of considerable embarrassment to both of us.

When I could run no more, I dropped to the ground, deciding I might as well let the bear eat me as run me to death. But the bear was gone. Perhaps he had taken a shortcut through the woods, hoping to cut me and Mr. Muldoon off at a pass. In any case, I never did get to see the bear, narrow as my escape had been. Sweltering in the fur coat, I took the thing off and stuffed it down a hollow stump, glad to be rid of the thing.

When I got back to camp, everyone was gone. I climbed up to the car, inside of which I found Eddie, his mother, and Goombaw, each more or less in one piece.

"Thank heavens," cried Mrs. Muldoon. "We thought the bear had got you! Have you seen Mr. Muldoon?"

I said yes I had, not mentioning that I had seen even more of him than I cared to. Half an hour later, Mr.

Muldoon scrambled up the bank to the car. Upon learning that everyone was intact, he explained how he had led the bear away from camp, at considerable risk to himself. I was surprised that he neglected to mention my role in leading the bear off, but didn't think it my place to mention it.

"You got to keep a cool head during a bear attack," Mr. Muldoon explained. "Panic and you're done for."

"Wheweee!" Goombaw said. "I smell skunk! Somebody step on a skunk in the dark?"

Then it started to rain. Hard.

Water Spirits

My first encounter with water spirits occurred at a high mountain lake in northern Idaho.
Dr. Mike Gass and I had grunted and gasped our way
up the steep, rocky trail to the remote lake on the basis
of rumors that large, savage cutthroat trout abounded
there.

As soon as we arrived, Mike set up operations on a
snow slide at one end of the lake, the only good casting
area. I wandered around the lake trying to find a place
I could cast from, but the shore was wrapped with a
thick fir collar right up to the water's edge. Finally I
came upon a slender log extending thirty feet or so into
the shallows. I did a balancing act out to the end of it
and frantically began tying on a fly.

Mike yelled gleefully about a big strike he had just
had. Glancing up to see if any fish were rising around
me, I noticed a V form near the middle of the lake, a
V such as a shark fin makes cutting the water, only tiny.
The V swept in a wide half circle and—much to my

astonishment—came right up to my feet! I stared down into the V to see what was making it, expecting a fish or maybe a large water bug of some sort. But there was nothing there! Nothing visible was making the V!

"Jeepers criminy," I said to myself. "There's nothing there."

While contemplating this curiosity, I glanced again out into the lake. Another V had formed. This one, too, swept in a wide half circle, only in the opposite direction. And it, too, came right up to my feet! I stared down into the V with considerable intensity, protruding my eyeballs for a better look. There was nothing in this V, either.

Being of a scientific bent, I carefully analyzed the situation, taking into account all possibilities for what might have caused the Vs and what could account for each of them to zoom right up to my feet. This process took no more than three seconds and led me to the only logical conclusion.

"Water spirits! Water spirits!" I yelled, rushing past Mike on my way to the trail.

Mike is a calm, practical, no-nonsense man, not easily budged in the direction of panic. Thus it came as no little surprise when he thundered past me on the trail, his fly line snapping like a whip in the wind. He claimed later that he didn't for one moment believe there were actually water spirits present, "because any person with an iota of intellect knows they don't exist." His haste, he explained, was due merely to the fact that he didn't want to be caught after dark in the mountains with a crazy person. It was clear to me that the lake contained water spirits, but I had no idea there was also a crazy person in the vicinity. Neither of us has returned to the lake since.

Several years passed without my having further confrontations with water spirits. I now shared a suite of offices with my friend Dick Hoover, a former television newscaster and a university professor. Hoov, as I call him, was now in the business of making films. I was writing magazine articles, spending hours every day hunched over a typewriter. One fine spring day, Hoov was bustling about in the outer office preparing to take a canoe trip down a nearby river to shoot some film of the flora and fauna. Thumping away on the typewriter, I thought, Why didn't I have the good sense to go into the filmmaking business so I, too, could be out canoeing on a beautiful day like this rather than being chained to a stupid typewriter?

Hoov left, and I continued to type away, pausing every few minutes to stoke my envy. A couple hours later, the door to the outer office slammed. I listened intently, wondering what irate being had just stormed in, and whether it might be after me. Then I heard footsteps: squish, squish, squish, squish. I got up and looked out. There was Hoov, streaming with water and spewing forth the rather mild, silent profanity he uses in extreme situations.

The canoe had tipped over and dumped him and all his camera gear into the river. An enormous wave of sympathy welled up in me, which I tried to conceal behind the façade of hearty laughter. Often this approach has the therapeutic value of showing the victim of such a mishap the lighter side of the misfortune, and the two of you end up having a jolly good time joshing each other. Occasionally, of course, it leads to one of those uncomfortable social situations in which the victim of the mishap fails to respond appropriately to humor and chooses instead to crush your windpipe.

Alas, the therapy failed to take hold on Hoov, who could think only of his filming gear resting on the bottom of the river, and whether throttling a laughing person might constitute a felony. Wiping away the feigned tears of mirth, I said, "By golly, Hoov, maybe all isn't lost. Maybe we can salvage some of your gear from the bottom of the river. I'll go get my canoe and make a grappling hook of some sort and we can drag the river. There's every chance that water and sand and gravel won't seriously harm expensive and delicate photographic equipment."

"I've paddled my last canoe," Hoov growled. "No, what we'll do is, I'll borrow a rowboat from my neighbor."

"Ha!" I said. "There's no way I'm going to go down that river in a rowboat. A person would have to be out of his mind to take a rowboat down that river!"

Hours later, Hoov was still in a wretched mood. "Row to the right," he commanded. "I think that's the spot I tipped over in."

"The sun's going down," I said. "And this is the forty-ninth spot you think you tipped over in. We'd better get out of here before it gets dark. It's a good three miles downriver to the take-out spot."

"Oh, let's try one more place," Hoov said.

"Listen," I said, "I didn't want to mention this before, but you know the reason you tipped over in the canoe?"

"Spare me," Hoov said.

"Water spirits," I said. "It was probably water spirits."

Hoov stared at me, the homemade grappling hook dangling ominously from his hand. Although I doubted he would grapple me, his stare made me a little nervous.

"You're crazy, McManus," Hoov said. "Water spirits!" For the first time that day, he laughed.

"I'm not kidding."

"I know you're not. That's why I say you're crazy."

"Oh yeah?" I said. "Well, Mr. Smarty, I did some research about the river, and back in the old days the Indians wouldn't go near this stretch because they believed it was inhabited by evil water spirits." It was true. I had actually read that, even though I didn't need research to support my conviction as to the presence of water spirits. Any fool could see that this creepy section of the river provided them with perfect habitat.

"Evil water spirits, indeed!" Hoov said, chuckling. "How do you come up with this kind of whimsical nonsense?"

"Think what you will," I said, "but let's get out of here just the same."

Hoov finally acquiesced to my demands and we drifted off downriver toward our car. The river was high with the spring runoff but generally placid, and I found it remarkably easy to steer the rowboat even going with the current. We zipped comfortably through several small rapids. Then we came to a stretch where huge trees reared up on both sides of the river, with an eerie evening light playing upon the water and patches of mist drifting about like stray ghosts out on a lark.

"I don't like the looks of this," I said.

"What?" Hoov said, seeing nothing but smooth water ahead of us.

"This place," I said. "It's quiet. Too quiet. Don't you realize this is a perfect place for evil water spirits to hang out?"

"Har har har har," Hoov laughed.

We drifted into a wide bend in the river. On the inside of the bend, a large thorn apple tree hung out over the water, raking the current with its branches. There was plenty of room to maneuver around it, so I didn't pay it much attention, preferring to sift the shadows of the woods around us for signs of hostile haunts.

"Har har har," Hoov laughed. "Har . . . ! Watch where you're rowing, McManus! We're headed for that thorn apple tree!"

There was still enough room to maneuver. I smiled at Hoov and dug the oars into the water. The boat failed to respond. I dug the oars in again. And again. Still no response. The oars were now whipping around like twin paddle wheels under full steam, but some Stephen King-ish force was drawing us irresistibly into the thorn apple tree, which—and I didn't imagine this, either—reached out for us with its gnarled, spiked limbs and drew us into its deadly embrace, hissing and grinning malevolently as it did so.

"McManus, you did this deliberately and . . . ARRR-HHHHHH!" Hoov leaped to his feet to fight off the thorn tree, which raked him fore and aft with its vicious claws.

Fortunately, we were both wearing life jackets. I dropped the oars and started to jump up to help Hoov fight the tree *mano a mano*. But something grabbed me from behind, and with enormous power, jerked me half out of the boat and slammed me flat on my back against the surface of the water.

"They've got me!" I yelled.

"Murphhh gragg zork!" Hoov cried. "Ow! Ow!"

I figured the water spirits had him, too.

All at once, we burst free of the thorn apple and floated gently off downstream. But the evil water spirits still held me flat against the surface of the water, still doing their best to pull me under.

"They won't let me go!" I yelled at the shredded

Hoov, who seemed to be deliberately ignoring my predicament. "The water spirits are trying to drown me!"

"Oh, for gosh sakes," Hoov said. "It's only the handle of the oar. When you dropped it, the oar went under the boat and the handle caught under your life jacket."

"I know that," I said, slipping my life jacket off the oar handle. "But don't try to tell me the evil water spirits had nothing to do with it."

Hoov glanced nervously over his shoulder. I could tell he was making an effort not to believe in water spirits. But they weren't done with us yet.

When we got to where we had parked the old station wagon Hoov used for his filming jaunts, we grabbed the boat, one of the few ever made of cast iron, dragged it up the bank, and shoved it into the rear of the wagon. With a last nervous glance at the river, we roared back toward town. I didn't want to raise the topic of water spirits with Hoov, but I had the eerie feeling a few of the more persistent haunts were clinging to the station wagon.

Presently, we heard a serious grinding noise in the back of the car. I looked at Hoov. I could tell he had leaped to the same conclusion I had.

"You want to stop and check out that noise?" I asked, hoping that Hoov would have enough sense not even to consider such a thing, particularly on a dark and lonely road.

"Better not," he said. "Maybe when we get back to town."

"Right," I said.

Upon arriving back in the city, we soon found ourselves trapped in six lanes of jammed-up traffic. We were on a well-lighted street, and this seemed like a good place and time to see what the water spirits had been up to with their grinding noise. Hoov opened his door and looked back. The left rear tire was on fire.

The left rear tire was not far from the gas tank.

The water spirits, having failed to drown us, were now trying to blow us up! I cursed the little buggers roundly, if briefly.

Hoov bounded out of the car yelling, "Fire! Fire! The gas tank is going to blow!"

The occupants of the cars wedged in tightly around us responded to this announcement with a good deal of interest. Previously, they had been slumped in their car seats staring morosely out the windshield at the impacted traffic, perhaps with no other thoughts on their minds than what a hard day they had had at the office. But now, with news of a gas tank about to explode mere feet away, they became suddenly animated and showed not the slightest sign of lethargy or fatigue. I myself had just accompanied three businessmen and two nuns in synchronized hurdles over several compact cars when I heard Hoov shout.

"McManus, stop! We've got to save the boat! It's not mine!"

Personally, I thought that was reason enough for not saving it, but Hoov insisted. We rushed back, grabbed the cast-iron boat, and, holding it over our heads to clear the tops of the cars, ran down the street with it, looking for a passage through the traffic jam. I have often wondered what the occupants of the cars two blocks away thought when they saw two panting middle-aged men running down the street at night carrying a cast-iron rowboat over their heads, particularly when one of them looked as if he had recently been fed through a pasta-making machine. With police and fire sirens converging from all sides, they probably thought we had stolen the boat, then forgotten where we had parked our car, and were making our getaway on foot.

By the time we got back to Hoov's station wagon, the fire department had arrived and extinguished the flaming tire. One of the firemen walked over to Hoov and asked him what had started the fire.

Hoov stood there quivering with exhaustion, his face and arms scratched by thorns and blackened by smoke, his shredded clothes still damp from the morning dunking in the river which had devoured all his filming gear, and he muttered, "A wheel bearing broke and overheated."

I'm not sure why he lied. Both of us knew what it really was that tried to get us, first with water, then with fire. On the other hand, maybe Hoov said the right thing. You never know how firemen might feel about water spirits.

Letter to the Boss

Mr. Clare Conley
Editor-in-Chief
Outdoor Life
New York, N.Y.

Dear Clare:
Good news! You know that expensive new
camera you thought you had lost on the Montana
fishing trip with me and Jim Zumbo? Well, it turned up.
It was still in the drift boat, wedged up under the bow
cover! Can you believe it?

I thoroughly enjoyed our little outing together. It was
a fairly typical fishing trip for me. Thank goodness! You
can imagine how nervous a fellow gets the first time he
takes his boss on an outing, no matter how commonplace
or trivial it might be. You just never know when something might go wrong. I have to chuckle every time I
recall your wondering aloud at the party in Kalispell the
night before whether it would be safe to go fishing with

me. Remember? You said, "All the crazy adventures McManus writes about, you sometimes wonder if some of them might actually be true. Wouldn't it be funny if he turned out to be as crazy as he writes!"

Boy, that line got a great laugh from everybody at the party. I'm sure all those present would have thought it just as funny if they hadn't been your employees. I for one thought it was a real thigh-bruiser. Anyway, I guess you know now that I am a fairly normal guy, even though my imagination does carry me away at times.

Oh, about the camera. As soon as it dries out, I'll rinse it good with gasoline to get rid of all the sand and rust. Then I'll send it off to you posthaste, because I'm sure you're anxious to see what kind of pictures it takes. I don't know much about photography but I suspect some of the pictures may have been damaged, because the film was sort of all lumped together and I probably scratched it quite a bit when I dug it out of the camera with a stick. I wasn't sure but I thought gasoline might affect the film adversely. Let me know if any of the pictures turn out, particularly the one of Zumbo's big fish.

I thanked Alan Christianson of the Rocky Mountain Elk Foundation and David Moles for loaning us the drift boat. Alan joked that he was just glad to get it back in one piece! Ha ha! You did hear that we found the boat, didn't you? It was hung up under a log a couple of miles downstream from the rapids. Ol' David knows how to build a sturdy drift boat. Aside from a few scratches, it was in great shape, even after being winched up the wall of the canyon.

The only other borrowed equipment we lost was one oar. You, of course, saved one of the oars by clinging to it even through the worst of the rapids. A less considerate and responsible person would simply have let the oar shift for itself, and would have struck out for the shore, although the canyon walls are so steep there you probably couldn't have got out anyway. Did you know that? You did the wise thing, which is to float a couple thousand yards down through the canyon, even if you had to spend half the time underwater. Better safe than sorry I always say.

You remember the life jacket you and I had that friendly little tug-of-war over just prior to capsizing? Well, even that turned up, on a gravel bar downstream from Bonners Ferry, Idaho. It still had the imprints of your fingers on it! Only kidding! Ha ha!

Even though you probably are aware of this, I should explain that I wasn't trying to wrest the life preserver from you, and I'm sorry if I gave you that impression. I was merely attempting to assist you in putting it on. I tried to tell you this at the time, but the roar of the rapids and Zumbo's screaming, "We're all gonna die! We're all gonna die!" probably drowned—unfortunate word that—out my voice, or maybe even caused you to think I had actually shouted something like "Give me that, you ——!"

Think about it. Would an employee shout something like that at his boss, particularly after he had just been promised a large raise? Sure, the raise involved the life preserver, although that certainly had nothing to do with my assisting you in putting the preserver on.

(By the way, the raise hasn't shown up on my paycheck yet. In fact, the paycheck hasn't shown up yet. Would you mention this to the comptroller?)

Don't be too hard on Zumbo. I realize that the little mishap was totally his fault, but keep in mind that he has written a lot of great stories for the magazine over the years. Still, after all the time he and I have kicked around together, he should have realized I don't know a thing about rowing a drift boat. Jim was certainly remiss in not arguing more forcefully that I not be allowed to row, because he more than anyone should have realized that my claim to having vast experience in handling drift boats in rapids was merely an attempt to introduce a little comic relief into the situation. Also, I thought it might take your mind off the treble-hook spinner dangling from your ear. And I guess it did that all right! Ha ha! Seriously, though, I think it would have been wise for you to let me remove the hook with my pocket knife, because, unlike drift-boat rowing, I do have vast experience removing hooks from ears and even more private parts of the anatomy.

Did I mention that Zumbo bumped my arm just as I was getting ready to make that cast? I don't think it was deliberate, but who can tell about Zumbo?

Please keep in mind that the whole idea for us to do a fishing trip together was Zumbo's. But, as I say, don't be too hard on him. He apparently didn't detect the jesting tone in your shouted threats when you chased him out of the canyon with the oar, which is probably why he lit out for the mountains immediately after the trip and hasn't been seen since. If by any chance you were serious about those threats, I will try to discover his whereabouts for you. What are friends for, I always say.

Any chance you can make it out West for a hunting trip with me this fall? My friend Retch Sweeney has offered to guide, if you could see your way clear to send five hundred dollars in advance so he can make bail. Don't expect any great amount of excitement. It would just be a typical McManus hunting trip. We'd love to have you along. Think about it.

And please, do stop by the comptroller's office and ask about my check.

Best regards,
Pat

Scritch's Creek

The first time I saw Ketchum Scritch I was
about twelve and spending the day with the old
woodsman Rancid Crabtree. Ketchum came driving up
in an ancient, rickety truck that seemed to be puffing
smoke from every orifice and portal. He was about as
tall a human being as I had ever seen, hard and sinewy,
with a week's growth of gray beard and coal-black eyes
glinting out of cavernous sockets. And there was a meanness to him, not the happy meanness of some people I
knew, but a serious, no-nonsense meanness.

In the truck with him was a little girl with wild tawny
hair and great wide blue eyes. She held a dog by the
collar. The dog curled a lip at me and growled. Ketchum
Scritch told the dog to shut up, and the dog did. I
thought probably Scritch could tell just about anything
to shut up and it would. He got out of the truck and
walked toward us carrying a gallon jug.

"Scritch," Rancid said.

"Crabtree," Scritch said.

Those were about the only two words exchanged between them. Rancid gave Scritch a wad of crumpled-up dollar bills and took the jug. Scritch got back in the truck and drove off in a cloud of smoke. I could see the little girl looking back out of the rear window of the truck.

After they had gone, I said to Rancid, "How come they call him Ketchum?"

"Wahl, it might be on account he come from Ketchum, Idaho. But Ah reckon it's 'cause if anybody does him a mean turn and tries to get away, he'll catch 'em. Ah recollect y'ars ago thar was a fella by the name of Ringo Dance who beat Scritch out of some money. The way Ah hear'd the story, Scritch caught up with him in a saloon in a little town up north. Ringo was standin' at the bar with some other men when Scritch stepped through the door and called out his name, mean and hard-like—*'Dance!'* Ringo jumped right out through a winder, and the other fellas, they took one look at Scritch and broke into a fox-trot. Ha! Ah guess they didn't know Ringo's last name was Dance."

I for one certainly did not want to be caught by Ketchum Scritch, whether or not I had done him a bad turn. Little did I know then what lay in store for me a few years hence.

"What's in the jug?" I asked Rancid.

"Some medicine ol' Scritch whups up fer me from time to time."

"Medicine? Why, you're never sick, Rancid."

"Thet jist goes to show what fine medicine it is," Rancid said, and he pulled the cork and took a dose of it. Then he gasped and wheezed and pounded himself on the chest. "Not only thet, it's good fer tannin' hides and curin' fence posts."

The next time I saw Ketchum Scritch was a couple

of years later. My friend Retch and I had hitchhiked back into the mountains with a couple of loggers to do some fishing. As we rounded a curve, the mountains opened up into a pretty little valley with a stream flowing through it.

"Hey, this looks like a good place," Retch told the loggers. "Just drop us off here and we'll spend the day fishin' that stream."

"You sure you want to fish there?" the driver said.

"Why not?" I asked. "You think it's fished out?"

"Naw," the other logger said. "I can almost guarantee you it ain't been fished a-tall." I caught him sneaking a wink at the driver.

"Then this is the place for us," Retch said. "We'd appreciate it if you'd pick us up on your way back tonight."

"Sure thing," the man who had winked said. "Leastwise we'll pick up as much as we can." Then the two loggers laughed for all they were worth. Looking back, I now realize that they were two of the happy mean type of people.

The fishing in that little stream was as fine as any I'd ever had. After we saw that we wouldn't have any trouble catching our limits, we dumped out our worm cans and started practicing our fly-fishing. It was beautiful the way those fat little cutthroat would tear into our Black Gnats, and every once in a while we would nail a twelve- or fourteen-incher, and once this huge redbelly flashed out from under a log and snapped my leader as if it were a cobweb. I told myself I'd have to come back and try for that fish again. It was one of those fish that swim forever in the dark currents of your mind, until you catch them. Then you eat them and forget them.

After Retch and I each had a good string of fish, we

stashed them and our fishing rods and went exploring. We walked down the middle of the creek singing and whistling and philosophizing, enjoying the cool, clinging wetness on our legs, the hot sun toasting our backs, and the creek itself, dappled with golden light beneath a veil of alder leaves. It was wonderful. Then I happened to notice a shed off to one side, almost concealed by honeysuckle.

"Why, look there," I said to Retch. "Somebody has built himself a little cabin."

"I'll be danged," Retch said. "Maybe it was built by an old prospector and he got froze to death or somethin' and left some gold nuggets layin' around. Let's go take a look."

As we scrambled out of the creek and started up the bank to the shed, a voice boomed, *"Whoa there!"*

We both whoaed. It was the sort of voice that if it had said "Dance!" you instantly would have broken into a fox-trot.

I looked around and there stood Ketchum Scritch. "What in tarnation you think you doin'?"

While I was still sorting through my hoard of lies for a good one, Retch stammered out, "W-why, we're uh lost. Yes, sir, we're lost!"

"Y-yeah," I said, picking up the cue. But before I could embroider the lie with some colorful and authentic details, Ketchum snatched Retch up by the shirt and held him straight out at arm's length. Retch's feet ran furiously in empty space.

"I don't know whether to skin you now or wait until the next time I catch you snoopin' around my property," Scritch said, looking as if he favored *now*.

"N-next time would suit me better," Retch whined, " 'cause there ain't gonna be no next time."

Then Scritch dropped him. Retch's feet being already revved up, he spun a couple of shallow furrows in the sod and then shot off through the brush, across the creek, and up the side of a mountain before I had even jammed myself into first gear.

Scritch looked down at me. "I seen your skinny carcass somewheres before," he said. "When I caught those poor fellas in here last year, you ain't by any chance the lucky one what got away, are ya?"

"N-no, sir," I said. "This is my first time, and I was just passing through, trying to find my way home."

"Well then, I want you to do just two things. The first is to pick up them fish you stashed up the crick."

"Y-yes, sir. And what's the other?"

"T'other is, *git!*"

After picking up the strings of fish, I set what might well have been the world's record for gitting. Retch and I were so scared that it was at least a week before we even thought about going back to fish Scritch's creek. It seemed such a shame, all those fine fat cutthroat going to waste. We began to speculate that maybe old Scritch was more bark than bite and decided to ask Rancid Crabtree his opinion.

"What age you be now?" Rancid asked.

"Fourteen."

"Wahl, then Ah wouldn't try fishin' thet crick ag'in, 'cause Scritch considers anybody over twelve a keeper."

"What's he use that old shed for, anyway?"

"Ah 'spect thet's whar he keeps the ones he don't throw back. You boys best steer clear of Scritch."

We didn't talk about fishing Scritch's creek anymore, but I couldn't get the thought of that huge, magical cutthroat out of my mind, the one that had snapped my leader. Several times in moments of fish madness I nearly sneaked back there, but the image of Ketchum holding Retch in the air at arm's length would shock me back to sanity. I was left with only my memory of that fine morning on Scritch's crick and a gnawing in my belly to fish it again.

A couple years passed, and I became almost as interested in girls as I was in fish. One Saturday Retch somehow managed to borrow his father's car, and he, Birdy Thompson, and I drove out to a little country school to a dance. Usually we went just to watch the Saturday Night Fight, in which a couple of the seedier characters at the dance would shuffle around each other in the parking lot, saying things like "So you think you can take me, hunh?" "I don't think, I know." "You and who else?" "I can take you with one hand tied behind me." "Yeah?" "Yeah!" And so on. They would shuffle around each other repeating these phrases for half an hour or so, hoping someone would jump in and say, "Okay, break it up, you guys." If no one said, "Okay, break it up, guys," then sooner or later they would have to roll around in the gravel of the parking lot for a while to satisfy the spectators who had stood around listening to all the boring chitchat.

But this Saturday night our plan was different. The idea, as I understood it, was to meet some girls and see if they wouldn't let us "take them home." I was a little nervous about the venture, because I didn't know that much about girls, and the very thought of actually "taking home" filled me with a secret dread. The dread was secret, because I had somehow managed to give the impression to the other guys—I don't know how—that I was an experienced ladies' man.

"Hoo boy!" Birdy said when we drove up to the school. "I got a feeling we're going to get lucky tonight!"

"Hoo boy," I said, wiping my palms on my good pants.

It turned out to be a pretty nice dance. Rancid Crabtree was there, whooping it up with his girlfriend, Ginger Ann. I danced a couple of dances with Ginger Ann, just to get loosened up a bit. She was soft and warm to the touch, and smelled nice, too, and pretty soon I was wondering if Rancid would mind if I took Ginger Ann home, just for practice.

"You got a ride home tonight, Ginger Ann?" I ventured.

"You bet I have, sweetie," she said. "Now why don't you go dance with that pretty little girl over there. Maybe she don't have a ride home."

Why, my eyeballs almost suffered cardiac arrest. Standing against the wall was about the cutest girl I'd ever seen, her tawny hair framing her big blue eyes, perky nose, and sullen mouth. I sauntered over to her. "Hi. My name is Patrick."

"So?"

"Uh, so, uh, I was wondering if you had, uh, a name."

"Sure I have a name! Pearly."

"Oh. Well, Pearly, would you go home with me? No! I mean, would you like to dance?"

Pearly practically leaped at the invitation. "Oh, I guess so," she said. My suavity had paid off.

I danced the next two dances with her, being very cool and sophisticated so she would know I was a man of the world. Every time I tried to ask her if she had a ride home, though, the words didn't come out right.

"Uh," I said to her suavely, "you must be getting very warm from all this dancing. You're sweating like a pig, ya know. Uh, do you have, uh, would you like, uh . . . some of that nice cool lemonade over there?"

"I sure would," she said. "I'd like to soak my sore feet in it."

Pearly may have been cute, but she had a bit of a mean streak, too.

As I was handing her a glass of lemonade is when the terrible misunderstanding occurred. Someone bumped me hard from behind, and I dumped the lemonade right down the front of Pearly's dress. Well, I was embarrassed and angry, and assumed the bump had been deliberate, a little practical joke perpetrated by either Retch or Birdy.

"Watch it, you moron!" I snapped. "Or I'll—"

"You and who else?"

Recognizing fighting words when I heard them, I slowly turned around. There stood a menacing mountain of bone and muscle that appeared to be, if not the missing link in the chain of human evolution, at least a misplaced one. He was a head taller than I and had real biceps, which looked like turtles doing pushups in his shirt sleeves.

"I want to go home," Pearly said, speaking my exact thought.

"Don'tcha wanta stay for the fight?" the link said to her.

"What fight?" I asked.

"The one between me 'n' you," the link said, thumping my chest with a finger the size of a cucumber. "Now let's go out to the parking lot."

Of all the possible destinations under my feverish consideration, the parking lot held such a low priority it didn't even register on the scale. But by now some interested spectators had gathered around us and were offering words of encouragement to both sides. With an audience looking on, I didn't feel I could resort to defensive groveling without at least going through the traditional fight ritual:

"So, you think you can take me, hunh."

This utterance so delighted and surprised my adversary that he burst out in a harsh laugh. "Yeah, I do."

"You and who else?"

Then I heard Birdy's voice whispering urgently in my ear. I hoped he had some plan for escape. "You know your new fly rod? I was wondering if, after the fight, I could . . ."

Suddenly, Rancid Crabtree was standing between Missing Link and me, shoving us apart. Wow, I thought, that was close. Now Rancid will say, "All right, you guys, break it up."

"All right, folks, Ah'm here to tell you this ain't gonna be no bloody spectacle put on for your amusement. You all jist go on about yer dancin' and let these fellas go out to the parking lot and settle their differences man-to-man in private. Ah'll go along jist to make shore it's a fa'r fight."

What? Is he stark-raving mad? This guy is going to kill me!

Rancid's little speech resulted in a good deal of disappointment, most of it apparently mine. Everyone else seemed to prefer dancing a polka to watching a poking. The last thing I wanted was a fight, fair or unfair making so little difference as to be inconsequential, because in either case I was going to get murdered.

The three of us walked out to the parking lot, the link rolling up his sleeves over his bulging biceps. I rolled up my shirt sleeves over where my biceps were supposed to be but hadn't yet put in an appearance. If they were ever going to show up, now was a good time.

"Fust thang," Rancid said, "Ah don't wanta see no eye gougin' or ear bitin' or puttin' the boots to a fella while he's down. Of course, it's okay while he's still standin' up." The link sneered, an expression I took as a clear indication he did not hold such sissy rules in high regard. "Now, Ah'm goin' to give each of you fellas a little tip about fightin'," Rancid went on, "since Ah've had considerable experience with it in maw day. But Ah better whisper it in yer ears so t'other fella can't hear it. You fust," he said to the link.

"I don't need no tip about fightin'," the link said. I believed him.

"You git it anyway," Rancid said, "because otherwise you might just end up beaten into a little pulpy mess that would make people sick to their stomachs just to look at you, and somehow folks might think Ah was to blame. Now, you don't want thet, do you, Harry?"

Harry? I thought. Rancid must know the link.

Rancid put his arm around where Harry's neck would have been if he'd had one, and started whispering. I could tell it must be very valuable information, because of the startled look on the link's face. All the time he was whispering, Rancid kept smiling and hugging Harry's head, which caused Harry to wince, and every once in a while they would look over at me, and the link would kind of shake his head in a little jerking motion. I was beginning to wonder if Rancid was giving my opponent a tip or a five-minute lecture in mayhem. Then a strange thing happened. Harry tore his head loose from Rancid's hug, scurried across the parking lot, leaped in his car, or somebody's car, and roared off down the road, spraying gravel over half the school playground.

Rancid stood there in the parking lot, hands on his

hips, rocking back and forth on the balls of his feet, smiling his big snaggle-toothed smile, and staring after the rapidly diminishing taillights.

"Shoot," he said. "Ah guess thet fella just remembered some bidness he had back in town. Thar won't be no fight after all."

I let out the breath I had caught when the link had first thumped my puny chest.

"What about my tip?" I said.

Rancid looked puzzled for an instant. "Oh, thet," he said. "Ah don't reckon you'll be needin' yer tip."

When Rancid and I walked back into the dance, a murmur of amazement drifted around the room. Rancid patted me on the back and turned to a group of men standing by the door. "Ah never seen nothin' like it," he told them. "Boy hits like a goldang pile driver! You'd never guess it, lookin' at them puny arms of his, would ya? Ah bet ole Harry don't stop runnin' till sunup tomorrow." The men all grinned, looking at my puny arms.

Retch and Birdy came over to congratulate me and said they knew I could hold my own with the link. "Yeah, and I was just foolin' when I asked about your fly rod," Birdy said. "I figured all along you could lick him. How come, do you suppose, Rancid wouldn't let anybody watch?"

"I don't know," I said. "It was pretty violent. I hope I didn't get blood splattered all over my good pants."

Suddenly, Pearly was standing in front of me. "You know what you went and done?" she said, her blue eyes flashing. "First you dumped lemonade all over my dress and now you beat up my ride home!"

"The link was your ride home?"

"He's my cousin is all—Harry Pitts!"

"Sorry," I said. "I didn't know."

"Well, now you're just gonna hafta take me home yourself."

"Hoo boy!" Birdy said, poking me in the ribs.

"Hoo boy is right," Rctch said, slapping me on the back. "I'll even loan you my old man's car. Don't mess it all up either. Ha!"

"Hoo boy," I said, my voice hardly cracking at all. This was not my night.

To tell the truth, "taking home" wasn't what it had been cracked up to be. Pearly sat hunched against the door on her side of the seat and devoted most of her attention to chewing a hangnail—the world's largest hangnail. Occasionally she would snap directions at me, but that was about all the conversation I could get out of her: "Turn there. . . . Take a left at the crossroads. . . . Go through that gate. . . ."

After half an hour, it occurred to me that we were getting pretty far into the mountains, and I was beginning to wonder if I could find my way back again. The road deteriorated into an overgrown pack trail, and I was tearing up brush and small trees with the bumper of Retch's old man's car.

"Holy cow!" I said finally. "How much farther is it, anyway?"

"Drive through that crick, smarty," Pearly snapped, "and we'll be nearly there." I imagined the look on Retch's old man's face if he could see me driving his car through a creek. It was pretty terrible.

A frightening thought suddenly hit me. Suppose Harry Pitts was at Pearly's house! Either I spoke the thought aloud or Pearly read my mind.

"Naw, Harry won't be there," she said. "It's my grampa's place. I'm stayin' with him for the summer."

We drove into a clearing at the far edge of which was a huge old log house. There was something about the place that caused the hair on the back of my neck to lift.

"Uh, this your Grandpa Pitts's place?" I asked.

"Naw," she said. "This here belongs to Grampa Scritch."

"Grandpa Scritch? *Scritch*? *SCRITCH!*"

As I simultaneously gunned the engine and attempted to push Pearly out the door, a great mean voice roared out, *"Whoa there!"* I had no trouble recognizing the voice. I stalled the engine just as Scritch himself stepped into the headlight beams.

"Now you gonna get it, I bet," Pearly said in her mean, squeaky little voice.

"Step out of that car, boy!" Scritch ordered. "What you doin' with Pearly? Get on up the house there, so's I can git a better look at you."

It soon became apparent that Harry had sneaked Pearly off to the dance without telling Grampa Scritch. By the time we got to the house, she was crying and saying that everything that had happened was my fault. I did not anticipate that the next few moments would be among my happier ones. I did not even anticipate there would be many next few moments. If Scritch had threatened to skin me over a few fish, what would he do to me for kidnapping his granddaughter? Worse yet, for *taking her home?*

Scritch turned up the lantern on the table and glared at me. "Now what's this all about?" he said.

"We-we-we-we," I explained.

"He whupped Harry!" Pearly blurted out. "And afterwards Harry run off and left me at the dance!"

"Whupped Harry?" Scritch boomed. "No!"

"Yeesssss!" whimpered Pearly.

"Good gosh almighty!" Scritch bellowed and brought his fist down so hard on the table the lantern flew up in the air almost as high as I did.

"S-sir," I said, "there may be some misunderstanding about that."

But it was too late. Scritch stepped around the table and came for me. I backed against a stove and shut my eyes. And then Scritch had me by the hand, crunching all my finger and knuckle bones into little splinters, and I supposed that he would then move on and do the same to the other parts of my body, one piece at a time. But then I realized he was pumping the remains of my hand up and down. He was shaking my hand! And laughing! I had never in my life heard even a rumor of someone's having seen Scritch laugh. Pearly seemed amazed, too. And, if I wasn't mistaken, disappointed.

"Laddy," he said after a bit, still squeezing the remains of my hand, "anybody who whups that no-good Harry Pitts is a friend of mine. If you can see your way clear, I'd like for you to whup his daddy, too." Then he laughed again. "Yup, from now on, laddy, you count yourself my friend. And old Scritch don't have many friends."

"That's h-hard to believe, sir," I said.

"It's true. And that's the way I like it!"

I thought it might not be too easy, being Ketchum Scritch's friend, but it was a darned sight more pleasant than being his enemy. After he had finished squeezing my hand, he poured Pearly and me each a glass of buttermilk and set out a plate of dry biscuits. I formerly had loathed buttermilk, but now found it to be far and away my favorite beverage. The dry biscuits tasted more delicious than the finest chocolate cake I'd ever eaten. Thus does a near brush with death heighten one's appreciation of the humbler things of life.

Scritch sat across the table from me, staring at my puny arms. "So you whupped Harry," he said. "Well, I be danged."

"I guess I better be going," I said. "There are a couple other fellows at the dance who might be needing the car."

"I like you," Scritch said. "I don't know why, but I do. If you want to take Pearly out again sometime, it's all right with me."

I looked at Pearly. She stuck out her tongue.

"Thanks anyway," I said, "but I'm more used to older ladies."

"I can understand that," Scritch said. "Anyway, if there's ever anything I can do for you . . ."

I stopped. My trembling, mangled hand rested on the doorknob. "There might be something," I said.

For many years afterwards, up until the time old Ketchum Scritch died, whenever I felt the urge to catch a mess of cutthroat trout, I had my own secret place, a mountain stream where golden light dappled the water beneath a fluttering veil of alder leaves.

I never saw either Pearly or Harry Pitts again, and as far as I was concerned, that was much too soon.

The Tin Horn

I have always made a point of avoiding violence, particularly if there's some chance I might become a participant in it. My father, on the other hand, was a professional fighter of sorts. He was paid money to box in Saturday matches promoted by hustlers in little Idaho logging towns, and he always won, even in the sissy fights where they used boxing gloves. My father loved boxing.

Dad tried to interest me in boxing from my earliest years, teaching me to jab with my left and hook with my right and step in for an uppercut. I enjoyed it. Then I found out the other guy got to hit back, and all the fun went out of boxing for me. Dad tried to conceal his disappointment, but I could sense a certain lack of enthusiasm when I would ask him to play paper dolls. He died when I was six. I've been sorry ever since that I hadn't faked as much interest in boxing as he did in paper dolls.

Life goes on. For my seventh birthday, one of my rich

aunts gave me a tin horn. "Lord," my mother muttered, "as if we didn't have trouble enough." She frequently made such irrational statements during those troubled days, and I thought the sooner I learned to play the tin horn the sooner I could cheer her up with a few little tunes. The horn had come with a book of sheet music. The composer of the music had chosen to use diagrams and numbers in place of notes, which was thoughtful of him, since I didn't know how to read music.

I loved that little tin horn and practiced on it day and night. The titles of the songs caught the mood of the music beautifully. For example, "Happy Little Blue Bird" went something like this: tah tah tah tah tah tah tah tah taaaaah. "Sad Little Rain Drop," by contrast, went: tah tah tah tah tah tah tah tah. Precociously, I mastered the entire book of songs in less than a week, although Mom said she thought surely it had been at least a year. "Nope," I replied, "just a week. And I've got them all memorized. Here, I'll play you 'Happy Little Blue Bird.' " Tah tah tah tah tah tah . . .

During the second or third week, one of the valves on the horn developed a squeak. Thus, "Sad Little Rain Drop" sounded like this: tah tah tah-squee tah tah-squee tah-squee tah . . . I asked Mom if she thought the squeak detracted too much from the music. She said no. The squeaky valve, however, was soon to play a major part in my young life and result in that rite of manhood so cherished in memory: one's first honest-to-goodness, no-holds-barred, knock-down, drag-out fight.

My worst enemy at the time, not counting my sister, the Troll, was a girl who lived on a nearby farm. Her name was Valvoleen Grooper. She was a year older than I, and a head taller. I sometimes played with Valvoleen's younger brother, Dicky, but because of his ever-lurking evil sister, I usually avoided him. One of Valvoleen's favorite sports was to snatch one of my playthings away from me and run and hide it. If I couldn't find it, too bad. I was losing some of my interest in paper dolls by then, so the loss didn't bother me much. It was the dishonor, the humiliation.

"You better give that back to me or I'll tell!" I'd scream at her.

"Tough tiddlywinks," Valvoleen would reply, and, with a haughty toss of her head, swagger off to her house.

As paper dolls began to lose their grip on me, they were replaced by fishing. Fortunately, a fine little trout stream ran through the back of our farm, and I had merely to dig a few worms, grab my fishing pole, and wander down to the creek anytime I felt like it, which was usually once or twice a day during the summer. With the arrival of the tin horn, however, and the discovery of my talent for music, fishing was momentarily forgotten. Then one day the horn turned up missing. I hunted high and low, far and wide for it, but the horn was not to be found.

"You seen my horn?" I asked Mom, who was relaxing at the kitchen table with a cup of coffee and the newspaper.

"Nnnph," she replied, with a casualness that showed little understanding of the significance of the loss. My whole musical career was at stake, and did she care?

"Maybe somebody stole it," the Troll said. "Good riddance, too!"

"Stole it?" I said.

"Yeah," the Troll said. "Somebody with a tin ear took your tin horn. Ha!"

"Would you two shut up," Mom said. "I'm trying to read the paper."

"Anybody been over here?" I said.

"Wha?" Mom said. "Oh, Dicky and Valvoleen stopped by while you were gone."

"Oh. But no hoboes or anybody who might steal a horn?"

"No."

I spent another day searching for the horn, trying to think of someplace outside I might have set it down, but to no avail. Finally, I gave up, dug some worms, and went down to the creek to fish. I caught a couple of six-inchers and some little ones. Even after the action slowed and finally stopped, I still sat there dangling the line in the water, thinking about my horn. I thought I could almost hear its melodious tah tah tah tah. Suddenly it occurred to me that I didn't just *think* I could hear the tin horn, I actually could hear it! Very faintly from somewhere upstream came the unmistakable notes of "Happy Little Blue Bird."

I tossed my fish pole up on the bank and ran upstream. As the music grew louder, I went into a crouch, sneaking silently along through the brush to the top of a bank where I could peer down unseen by the horn player. I had not formulated any plan yet for retrieving the horn, mainly because I expected to see a large, dirty hobo playing it. Crawling on my belly, I parted the grass at the top of the rise. There, down below me, sitting on a grassy spot by the crick, was Valvoleen. She was now playing "Sad Little Rain Drop" but without the subtle melancholy I could evoke from the song. Tah tah tah-squee tah tah-squee tah-squee tah . . . The squeak! Now there was no doubt that the horn was mine. Valvoleen had stolen it. I was consumed with rage.

But restraint was called for. I needed a strategy. I knew from experience that Valvoleen could outrun me.

I would have to get close, then snatch the horn from her before she knew what was happening.

I stood up, brushed off the front of my shirt and jeans, and sauntered down the slope to the creek, whistling as I went. Valvoleen saw me, her eyes narrowing to slits, but she continued to play, if somewhat raggedly, on the horn.

"Oh, Valvoleen," I said, moving closer. "Fancy seeing you here."

Valvoleen took the horn from her lips. "Beat it, Dumbo. Don't you see I'm trying to practice my music?"

"Oh, yeah, I see that." I moved closer. "Very pretty." A few more feet. She was standing up, suspicion tightening the skin around her mouth and eyes. "I was just up the crick fishing when I heard this pretty music and wondered who . . ."

I lunged for the tin horn, got one hand on it.

"You stupid little wart!" screamed Valvoleen. "What are you doing?"

I jerked at the horn. "It's mine! You stole it from me!"

"Did not! It's mine!" Her left jab caught me square on the nose. I staggered back, trying to think of a suitably sardonic comment, but all I could come up with was the traditional and mundane "Owwwwww!" Valvoleen had broken my grip, not to mention probably my nose. She darted for the path up the bank, but I cut her off. She backed away, keeping her lethal left fist cocked high. I moved in. She backed away. Both of us were breathing hard. A large gray cedar log slanted out across the creek behind her. Valvoleen jumped to the log. A tactical error. Now I had her.

I jumped to the log. She backed up to where the log slanted down into the water. There was no place for her to go now. She would have to stand and fight. She stuck the horn down through the belt in her jeans and came at me, fists high, feinting with the left. I went in under the right hook I knew was coming and tried for an uppercut. I missed her chin but grazed an ear, almost dislodging her glasses. Bad timing. If I'd knocked off her glasses I would have had her. Valvoleen responded with a kidney punch, or at least a punch on some kind of organ that hurt like mad. Then she kneed me solidly but to no effect. I slipped and went down, getting in a lucky kneecap punch, right on the crazy bone. She howled satisfyingly. I whipped an ankle hold on her. She responded with the old but effective hairpull, permanently inverting several hundred of my follicles. I could hardly breathe. Then I realized it was because my face was being pressed down into the log. Valvoleen had released her hairhold and was kneeling on my head while giving me body shots to the ribs. I was beginning to lose interest in music. Finally, with every last ounce of my seven-year-old strength, I drew my left leg up under me and with a powerful thrust toppled us both into the water.

Valvoleen came up wide-eyed and choking. "Save me!" she cried, thrashing about. "I can't swim!"

I stood up. The water was only up to my hips. I grabbed her by the back of the collar and dragged her to shore in the manner made fashionable by John Wayne. I reached down and took my tin horn from her belt.

"Let that be a lesson to you," I said, and walked off up the hill. I shook the water out of the tin horn and began to play "Happy Little Blue Bird": tah-squee tah-squee tah-squee . . . When I got to the top of the hill, I turned and looked back. Valvoleen was still sitting in the water at the edge of the crick. Her chin was on her chest. I thought she might even be crying. I smiled. Dad would have been proud of me. Tah-squee tah-squee tah-squee tah-squee . . .

When I got home, the Troll met me at the door. "Guess what? I found your horn. It was rolled up in a newspaper in the back of Mom's closet. How much will you give me to get it back? How come you're all wet? Yuck! You've had a nosebleed! You look like you've been in a fight. And where did you get that other horn?

"Valvoleen," I said. "It's Valvoleen's. I'm just borrowing it."

I felt a little bad about accusing Valvoleen of stealing, then beating her up and taking her horn. So the next day I gave the horn back to her. Well, I didn't exactly give it back. I hid it and let her look for it.

Cupidity, Draw Thy Bow

My first real, honest-to-goodness date ever was with Melba Peachbottom, far and away the loveliest girl in seventh grade at Delmore Blight Junior High. I personally thought the date a great success, but Melba, for some obscure reason, found it less than satisfactory, or so I assume from the fact that she has not spoken a word to me in the forty years since.

I realize now that part of my fascination with Melba consisted in her newness. The girls I had gone to school with through grade school were all attractive in their own way, but they lacked the mystery of the unknown. There was my good friend Olga Bonemarrow, for example, but after six years of suffering through the same sights, sounds, and smells, particularly the smells, of grade school, what was there to talk about? The time we nearly froze to death because all the classroom windows were kept wide open after Stink Miller trapped his first skunk? Or, more intimately, the time I hit Olga in the ear with a spitball intended for Retch Sweeney, and it stuck right there in her ear until she dug it out with a pencil? I don't know why, but there was just something about hitting a girl in the ear with a spitball that tarnished her for me, at least as a candidate for first date.

Melba, on the other hand, was shiny new, with unmercifully blue eyes and tawny hair and an actual figure. I knew that female figures were highly prized by older men, and even though I was primarily interested in pretty faces, I thought Melba's having a figure probably counted as a plus. Even on the first day of school I noticed she was attracted to me. Once I even caught her looking in my direction, daintily covering a yawn with her cute little hand. Our relationship developed rapidly over the next couple of weeks. Then it turned serious and soon after that got totally out of hand. At the rate this wild, impetuous affair was rushing tumultuously along, I knew the moment was fast approaching when I would actually have to—oh, sublime agony!—speak to her.

Cripes! Sure, I was as suave and sophisticated as the next twelve-year-old at Delmore Blight, and undoubtedly I had the finest pompadour in the entire school. Each morning I would coat my hair with this hair-dressing goop I had got from my beautician cousin, Elmira. Then with great delicacy and attention to detail I would mold my hair into loops and waves and rolls until the pompadour covered the whole top of my head and violated considerable airspace on both sides and above. My ears looked like two helpless little pink things caught in a raging brown surf. With possibly the world's greatest pompadour going for me, I didn't see how I could miss with Melba. Still, there was that formidable obstacle—speaking to her for the first time. Cripes!

What kind of opening could I use? I couldn't very well just walk up to her and say, "Hi, Melba," because I sat scarcely three feet away from her every day of the week. She was always sitting right there—radiantly there—practically at arm's length. How could I suddenly, for no reason, blurt out, "Hi, Melba," as though I had just happened to run into her at a swank cocktail party or something? My one hope was that during lunch recess she would almost get run over by a logging truck, and I could shout, "Watch out, Melba!" That would break the ice. Unfortunately, a truck never came within a hundred yards of her. If one even came as close to her as fifty yards, I was ready to shout my warning, but none ever did. Even to get a shot at Melba, a truck would have had to drive halfway up the fire escape, because every lunch hour she sat up there with her girlfriends, whispering and giggling. Melba was driving me crazy, and I began to think she avoided trucks just to spite me.

As my mentor, the old woodsman and man of the world Rancid Crabtree, was fond of saying, faint heart never won fair maiden. I decided to take the bull by the horns. As might be expected, I got gored. Despite my suave, sophisticated manner, I suffered from a slight speech impediment whenever I got nervous. I stuttered. Since I seldom got nervous, few of my schoolmates realized I was thusly afflicted. I had decided to go with the basic "Hi, Melba," even though I knew it sounded stupid. But if I could just initiate the conversation, she would probably reply, "Hi, Patrick, how are you today?" and I would say, "I'm just fine, Melba. And you?" and she would say, "I'm fine, too," and I would say, "How about a date next Saturday?" Cripes! I could feel sweat streaming down my back as I sauntered up the fire escape toward Melba and her friends. Fire escapes aren't that easy to saunter up, either.

Suddenly, there I was, hovering over Melba and her friends, all of whom stared at me in wondering and electric silence. I was committed now. I couldn't very well say, "Excuse me. I'm just passing through on my way to the top of the fire escape." There was nothing to do but blurt out "Hi, Melba," and that is what I attempted. But all that came out was, "Hu-hu-hu-hu-hu-hu . . ." Cripes!

Janie McAllister, one of the friends, immediately took matters into her own hands and extricated me from the predicament. She leaned over the edge of the fire escape and yelled at the school-ground supervisor: "Mrs. Grendel! Patrick's panting on us!"

"Patrick!" screamed Mrs. Grendel. "Get down off that fire escape and stop tormenting those girls!"

Trying to make the best of a bad situation, I laughed evilly and fled.

Whether it was my suave, sophisticated manner or the pompadour that impressed Melba, I'll never know, but the very next day she actually spoke to me. I was standing casually—I always stood casually in those days—next to the water fountain when Melba walked right up to me and said, "Excuse me. I'd like a drink." I stepped aside with a flourish, grasped the faucet knob, and suave as Cary Grant cracked, "It's on me, Melba." In a spasm of nerves, I then turned the knob too hard and squirted approximately a quart of water up Melba's nose. If ever a romance was ill-fated, this was it! Cripes! I laughed evilly and fled.

I naturally concluded that the water-faucet debacle had permanently fractured our relationship, but that afternoon, as I casually wallowed in the black pit of despair, Melba suddenly, miraculously penetrated the gloom and asked if she could borrow a sheet of tablet paper. From my ceaseless surveillance of every detail of her classroom existence, I knew that Melba had practically a whole tablet tucked away neatly in her desk. "Uh, sure," I quipped. At that moment I knew with certainty that I would never solve the intricate and lovely jigsaw puzzle that was Woman. Too many missing pieces. But what the heck.

Immediately after school, I asked Melba if she would go on a date with me the following Saturday. She hesitated, possibly pondering whether I was about to laugh evilly and flee. But then her pent-up emotion for me burst its restraints and gushed forth. "Okay," she said.

A first date for a twelve-year-old boy is knotty with problems, not the least of which is how to transport the girl to the place where the date is to occur. As expected, my parents showed great reluctance to loan me the family sedan, and I was not about to risk the humiliation of having one of them drive us to and from the date. (Both my parents were a terrible embarrassment to me at the time, although they improved enormously with age.) My only other option was to carry her on my bike. If Melba thought that too awkward, she could perhaps walk alongside the bike, while I pedaled slowly. I guessed that she would prefer to ride, and in preparation for that likelihood I attached one of my mother's decorative pillows to the rear-fender carrier. Melba, sensitive soul that she was, would probably appreciate this thoughtful touch.

Saturday, I knocked nervously on Melba's door and was invited in by Mr. Peachbottom. He seemed pleasant enough. "Hello, son," he said. "Here, let me take your hat."

"I'm not wearing a hat, sir," I replied.

"You're not?" he said, taking a pair of spectacles from his shirt pocket and putting them on. "Oh. Sorry. Very nice pompadour you have there."

"Thanks."

At that moment, Melba floated radiantly into the room wearing a nifty pink dress.

"You look nice," I said.

"Gee, thanks," she said, blushing.

"Well, well, well," said Mr. Peachbottom, beaming. "Where are you two kids off to? Harold's Ice Cream Emporium, I suspect."

Melba gave me one of her dazzling smiles as she awaited my response.

"Oh no, sir," I said. "Something much more exciting than that."

"Indeed," said Mr. Peachbottom. Melba's smile increased by about fifty watts.

"Yeah," I said. "Hogg Slough! Bass fishing! I caught a beaut out there last week. Almost three pounds. But I'm pretty sure there's some five-pounders in there, too. I brought an extra pole for you, Melba, and a whole big glob of nice fat lively night crawlers. Ever catch a bass before?"

Melba shook her head.

"No? Well, this will be a real treat for you then."

I guess I was pretty well off the mark with that prediction, about bass fishing being a treat for Melba. After the date, she never spoke to me again, nor much during it. Thus do romances bloom and flourish and as quickly wither away.

The next weekend, Olga Bonemarrow and I took my bike and went out fishing at Hogg Slough. Olga wasn't as pretty and mysterious as Melba Peachbottom, but she was a whole lot better bass fisherman. I felt comfortable with Olga, too, and didn't have to put on airs. Even so I did regret removing the pillow from the rear-fender carrier, which I knew could get hard and uncomfortable on a long ride.

"Pedal a little faster, Bonemarrow," I told Olga. "My rear end is getting sore."

Whitewater Fever

I was tunneling through my garage the other day when my irascible neighbor, one Alphonse P. Finley, popped in, demanding to know the whereabouts of his lawn mower.

"Ye gods," he exclaimed in mock alarm. "What a mess! Aren't you afraid of getting buried in an avalanche in here?" Finley is a tidiness-excessive personality.

"Don't raise your voice so loud," I said. "Sound vibrations can sometimes trigger a slide up by the rafters. Also, I'd prefer it if you didn't bother me now. I'm looking for a saw."

"You'll never find it in here."

"It's a table saw," I said, probing gently into a pile with a wading staff. "Maybe it's under those canoes. Give me a hand and we'll move the canoes outside."

"I didn't come here to help you eviscerate your garage. I just want my lawn mower."

"Maybe it's under the canoes, too," I said shrewdly.

As Finley and I were lifting the top canoe, he clumsily

bumped a paddle, which nudged some tent poles, which in turn dislodged an amorphous yellow blob from the top of my fishing-rod cabinet. The blob plummeted down, enveloping Finley.

"Aulp! Aulp!" he yelled, muffling his panicky cries with the rubberized fabric.

"No need for concern," I said. "These old World War Two surplus life rafts are pretty tough. I doubt you could hurt one with your head."

Finley dumped the raft off him, wiping dust and cobwebs from his wispy pate. "Yeech! Nasty! A raft, you say. Don't tell me you actually trusted your life to this thing on water."

"Oh yes indeed," I said. "Retch Sweeney and I were among the pioneer river rafters of the Pacific Northwest. Haven't used it in a while, though."

Twenty-five years, in fact. The last time I'd used the raft was when Retch Sweeney, his dog, Smarts, and I shot the Chick-n-out Narrows in the middle of the night.

We had not intended to shoot the Narrows in the middle of the night, or any other time for that matter. We were unfamiliar with the river, but people who knew it had told us, "Watch out for the N-N-Narrows! Watch out for the N-N-Narrows!" Then an old rancher who ran cattle up along the river informed us that the Narrows were greatly overrated and told us where they were located. As we discovered later, either the old rancher didn't know which narrows we were interested in or he was a homicidal maniac. I still favor the latter.

Assuming we had already passed through the danger spot, a timid chute of water, Retch and I decided to float out of the canyon one evening, expecting nothing more then a serene, moonlit float down to our take-out spot. The dog, Smarts, stupidly went along with the plan.

As we bobbed sleepily along through the night, we were suddenly startled into full alertness by a yelp of alarm from Smarts. The dog's tail, ears, and hair stood straight out from his body, as though some malicious practical joker had just plugged his tail into a light socket. We instantly ascertained his cause for alarm, which served to dampen our mirth over the dog's comic electrification: the river had turned up on its side and was squeezing itself through an ever-narrowing corridor of rock walls! Even worse, at the end of the corridor, the river appeared to flow directly into a tunnel it had gouged into the mountain.

Dispensing with any discussion of the possible geological causes of this phenomenon, we took to our paddles and expended considerable energy in trying to paddle the raft upstream. But to no avail. As we were swept toward the entrance to the tunnel, the hideous roaring intensified until it became almost deafening. Typical of such predicaments, however, our roaring did no good at all and only contributed to our sense of unease, which was reaching levels never before detected in human beings.

Years later I returned to the Narrows to observe it in daylight, and discovered that it was not a tunnel at all but a channel cut in a twisting, dropping course down through solid rock and so narrow that a rafter going through it could reach out and touch both sides simultaneously. There was nothing left to indicate the magnitude of our terror as we were sucked through the Narrows in the dark of that dreadful night, except the marks where four sets of human fingernails and a pair of dog claws had scratched along the granite walls. I was surprised to see that the scratch marks had already eroded away until they were now scarcely an eighth of an inch deep. Thus does nature erase the puny works of man and dog.

The experience took a lot out of Smarts. Afterwards he went about with an empty look and a wild, haunted stare, all the more poignant for his having had most of the hair worn off him in the Narrows. A few weeks later, however, he returned to his same old self, which was no great improvement. The only residual effects Retch and I suffered were that we stuttered over the word "Narrows" and went about for some time afterwards with an expression of absolute horror frozen on our faces. This was particularly embarrassing in restaurants and at dinner parties. "Oh my, what is it?" a hostess would ask me. "The asparagus soup?"

"No, ma'am," I'd explain. "Just the N-N-Narrows."

For twenty-five years I had blocked the Narrows, and the raft, out of my consciousness. And now it had flopped down on Finley, as if once again vying for my attention.

"You know what?" I said to Finley. "You and Retch Sweeney and I should haul this raft up the St. Joe and have ourselves a little float trip. Nothing risky or anything—just a pleasant little one-day float down a gentle river."

"Ha!" Finley snapped. "You must be mad! To think that I for even one moment would consider floating down a river with that stupid, ugly thing!"

"Well sure, it's a little ugly right now, but once it's inflated it looks pretty good."

"I was referring to Sweeney. But ditto your raft."

Driving up the St. Joe with the bundled raft lashed to the top of the car, Retch and I couldn't help but chuckle at how Al Finley had ridiculed our little adventure. Retch mimicked Finley's shrill voice: "A watery grave, that's what I would expect of your little float trip!"

"Funny," I said between appreciative chortles. "And what was it he said about nincompoops?"

"I said," Finley's shrill voice replied from the backseat, "that I would have to be totally out of my mind to float a river with you two nincompoops. What possessed me to come along I'll never know."

"It was your spirit of adventure," I said. "Also, you wanted to hear all the bad things we would say about you."

"Yes, well, I would think you would at least speak decently of a person suffering from temporary insanity."

"Listen, Finley," Retch said, "this is nothing more than a simple little float, not much more exciting than playing with your rubber duck in the tub. You want excitement, you should have floated with us in the old days. That was excitement!"

"And terror," I said.

"Yeah, and terror."

River rafting, of course, has improved considerably since those days. I told Retch and Finley about a recent float trip I'd taken down the Moyie River with my friend Peter Grubb, whose River Odysseys West in Coeur d'Alene, Idaho, of all places, runs float trips all over the world. Peter's lecture on safety lasts almost as long as the trip. I was particularly attentive to Peter's instructions on what to do when tossed out of the raft: lie on your back with your legs pointed downstream so you can see where you're going, while backstroking with your arms to steer toward the nearest landing spot on shore. This varied somewhat from my own method, which consisted of running as fast as I could over the surface of the water.

"Tell me that again," Finley said. "Grubb's version."

I did. "Also, Peter introduced me to some great new rafting equipment, like these little electric pumps that run off a car battery and can inflate a raft in about three minutes. It used to take Retch and me hours to pump up a raft with a tire pump. Boy, modern technology sure can take the work out of rafting. Mostly, though, Peter is a safety fanatic. He says he never runs a river without scouting it first. That's what we're doing now, Finley, scouting the river from the road."

"Indeed? Well, how about where the river curves away from the road here and goes through that canyon? Shouldn't we stop and scout that?"

"Don't be a sissy, Finley," Retch said. "What would the river be doing in that canyon that it isn't doing here? Har har!"

"Right," I said. "Har har!"

An hour later we were floating down the river. I took up the captain's position in the bow, while Retch paddled from the stern. Finley sprawled in the middle of the raft, doing his impression of a limp washrag.

"I thought you said you had one of those new electric raft inflators," he gasped.

"Nope. Still just a tire pump. But you'll get the hang of it after you pump up the raft a few more times. I thought you were starting to catch your rhythm there towards the end."

The float was about what we expected: the gentle bobbing motion of the raft, birds twittering along the banks, trout darting away from the raft, deer staring in awe at the strange yellow creature drifting by. I popped the tab on a can of diet root beer as we drifted pleasantly away from the road and into the canyon.

"What's that noise?" I said. "Sounds like a train. Surely the train doesn't run through this canyon."

"Gee. It sounds like the train is wrecking," Retch said. "Almost reminds me of the N-N-N-N . . . !"

We swept around the next bend, the river picking up momentum. Then we saw why. It was getting a run at a series of high hurdles and a high jump, followed by a pole vault. When we plummeted down from the crest of the pole vault, I glanced back to see if Retch and Finley were still aboard. Both of them had their mouths stretched wide open. I think they may have been screaming, but the thunderous roar of the water drowned them out. I turned to see what they might be screaming about and discovered that the river had bunched up in a big, boiling knot and then thrust itself straight up into a towering wall of water curling back at the top. We swooped up under the curl and hung there, slipping up and down and back up the steep green slope of the wave. At that moment, I noticed that the wave was fairly thin up near the top, so I poked my head through it and took a look downstream. The next fifty yards looked like more of the same. After that, though, the river turned mean.

Two years later we emerged from the canyon. It was the longest time I'd spent on a raft since the N-N-Narrows. Retch was gasping for air as he knocked the water out of his ears. Finley was lying on his back with legs pointed downstream and backstroking with his arms.

"Knock it off, Finley," I said. "You're still in the raft. Did I forget to mention you're supposed to keep your eyes open?"

"What?" Finley said. "We're alive? I can't believe it!"

"Let this be a lesson to you," I said. "Always scout a

river before you float it. How many times do I have to tell you? Everybody okay?"

"I'm fine," Retch said. "Swallowed about five gallons of water is all, but that shouldn't bother me none. The river couldn't possibly be polluted way up here."

"Speak for yourself," Finley said.

"I'm all right, I think," I said. "I've got this big lump in my throat, probably just from fear. On the other hand, it could be a can of diet root beer. How about you, Finley?"

"I don't think I'm injured, but my face feels funny," Finley said. "Anything wrong with my face?"

"Nothing serious," I said. "You've just got a look of absolute horror frozen on it. It'll wear off after a few weeks. Just stay away from restaurants and dinner parties in the meantime."

Never Cry "Arp!"

I have long maintained that it is not the fish caught nor the game shot that makes the outdoor life so satisfying but the miseries endured in the course of those endeavors. I was first introduced to the satisfaction of outdoor miseries by my good friend Crazy Eddie Muldoon, who, at age eight, was a sort of magnet to injuries. It was almost as though Eddie scheduled his injuries for the day when he got up in the morning.

8:00	Stub big toe of left foot.
8:35	Step on rusty nail with right foot.
9:05	Get stung over left eye by bee.
10:30	Run sliver in hand while whittling.
10:35	Cut finger while whittling.
11:00	Twist ankle jumping off pigpen fence.
11:22	Get tick embedded behind left ear.
12:00	Lunch.
1:15	Get stung by nettles.
2:00	Get bitten by the Petersons' dog.

And so on throughout the day. I never knew there were so many injuries to be had until I met Crazy Eddie. There were burns, bangs, bites, breaks, cuts, conks, fractures, gouges, hits, knocks, punctures, pulls, pinches, scrapes, scratches, smashes, stings, stubs, strains, sprains, whacks, wrenches, and wallops.

And more. By the end of a day, Eddie would acquire most of them. He would go home with a series of tear flows recorded in the dirt on his face, like the various flows of lava from a volcano. There would be the eleven-o'clock twisted-ankle flow stopped just short of the two-o'clock dogbite flow. A geologist could read the day's events on Eddie's face.

It was Eddie who taught me never to cry over an injury, no matter how painful. He said you were just supposed to laugh it off. For instance, once Eddie was banging two big rocks together to see if there were any gold nuggets inside, and one of his fingers slipped between the rocks. The distinctive sound still sticks in my mind: *WHOCK WHOCK WHOCK whib* "*Aaaaaaaiiiiii!*" Eddie hunched over and hopped around with his flat finger clutched in his crotch, performing a variation of the adult outdoorsman's traditional crouch hop, but more agile and much faster, like a basketball being dribbled at blurring speed. He also emitted strange, high-pitched sounds.

With much concern, I studied Eddie's face for signs of tears. "Hey, you're crying, Eddie. You got tears runnin' down your face."

"Hiii-yiiii! Ow ow!" he yelled. "No I ain't! Owwwww! Ha ha! Owwwww! Waaaa! Ha ha! See, I'm laughing it off. Oww! Waaa! Ha ha! Haaiiii!"

"I think you're crying."

"Nope, I'm not."

"Oh, sorry, I thought you was."

"Nope."

I never knew Eddie when he had all of his fingernails whole and healthy. Most of them would be in various stages of coming or going, either shiny pink little nubbins or hideous black things.

"Hey, this fingernail is about to come off," he would tell me. "Want to see me peel it?"

"Sure."

"Ouch! There. What did you think of that? I got another one about ready to peel, too. I'll let you know when it's time."

I never told Eddie, because I didn't want to hurt his feelings, but watching him peel off his fingernails wasn't all that entertaining. It lacked the suspense of his slowly unwrapping a bandage so I could see one of his nastier wounds.

Usually, Eddie accumulated his injuries sequentially. But on one occasion he got them all at once. We were roaring down a steep hill on our bicycles when Eddie's bike chain ate his pant leg. At the same time, a hornet traveling at supersonic speed hit him right between the eyes. Eddie was knocked backwards right off his bike. He and the bike bounced and smashed and crashed on down the hill, until at last they both racked up in a pile against a signpost. I braked to a stop on one of his arms. Eddie didn't seem to notice. He and the bike looked as if they had been wadded up and tossed out the window of a passing car. Well, I thought, if I'm ever going to see Eddie cry, this is it.

He didn't cry, though. He just lay there in a tangle of bicycle, saying something that sounded like "Arp arp

arp." I pulled his pants leg loose from the bike chain, got him astraddle of the rear-fender carrier on my bike, and pedaled him toward his house.

"Feel like playing some more, or you want to go home, Eddie?" I asked him.

"Arp arp arp," he replied. So I took him home.

I dumped him off the bike in his yard and he just lay there on the grass. I figured I could leave him there, and sooner or later his mother would find him. If I stayed, I'd have to explain how it all happened and how it wasn't my fault and all the other nonsense required on such occasions.

"Arp arp arp," Eddie said to me.

"Oh, all right," I said. "I'll go tell your mom." For all his shortcomings, Eddie had a way with words.

I knocked on the door, and Mrs. Muldoon called out for me to come into the kitchen. She smiled at me, wiping her hands on her apron. "Land sakes, Patrick, where did you get all those scratches on your face?"

"Eddie and me was climbing a thorn apple tree."

"Well, you're certainly a mess."

"Yeah, but wait until you see Eddie."

"Oh, that boy! He's always getting himself so banged up. But he never cries, does he?"

"Nope. But he says 'Arp arp arp' a lot."

" 'Arp arp arp'? Say, would you like a cookie and a glass of milk?"

"Yes, ma'am."

Mrs. Muldoon poured two glasses of milk and set them on the table with a little pile of sugar cookies beside each. I dipped a cookie in my glass of milk and bit off the soggy portion. There was a well-established technique for eating sugar cookies with milk. The cookie was too big around to fit all the way into the glass. So you dipped an edge of it as far as it would reach into the milk. Then you ate off that edge. Next, you turned the cookie over and dipped the opposite edge in the milk and ate it off. Now the cookie was narrow enough to fit all the way down into the glass, and you could dip it and eat it in two bites.

Mrs. Muldoon smiled at me. I could tell she knew a skilled milk-and-sugar-cookie eater when she saw one. "Where's Eddie?" she asked. "Isn't he coming in?"

"Oh, I nearly forgot," I said. "Eddie got hurt."

"Oh dear, that boy! He is always getting himself so banged up. What is it this time? His big toe? Another finger?"

I expertly finished off a second sugar cookie. "I don't know for sure," I said, "but to me it looks pretty much like all of him."

Mrs. Muldoon walked to the door and looked out. "Good heavens! Eddieeeeee!! What happened to you?"

Faintly, I heard Eddie's answer. "Arp arp arp."

I pocketed his sugar cookies and left. He probably wouldn't feel much like eating them anyway.

The next day I rode over to Eddie's house to see if he could play. He was in bed in his pajamas, with bandages sticking out the legs and sleeves. One of his ankles was as big as a grapefruit—a spoiled grapefruit. Both his eyes were black and blue, and swelled shut, except for a narrow slit in one eye. I could see him peering at me out of that slit.

"I didn't cry, did I? If you say I did, you're lying."

"You didn't cry," I said. "A lot of guys would have cried, but you didn't. Any more than I would have."

Eddie leaned back on his pillows and smiled with satisfaction. "That was a terrific crash, wasn't it?"

"Yeah," I said. "The best I ever seen."

"Look at these eyes and my ankles. They're awful, ain't they?" He grinned. "Norm and Jackie and Kenny are all coming over this afternoon to look at me. Boy, I bet I almost make them sick."

"You almost make me sick," I said.

"Really? You're not just saying that? Hey, listen, I'm gonna get some terrific scabs out of this. When they get ready, you can come over and watch me peel 'em off. Okay?"

"Yeah, sure," I said. "Well, I gotta go. See ya later, Eddie."

Pedaling my bike back home, I couldn't help but feel depressed. There was poor Eddie in bed, all stung and sprained and cut and bruised and scraped practically to pieces. I couldn't understand why it had happened to him, my best friend. Some guys had all the luck.

Visions of Fish and Game

Much study has been done on how fish and game see. For example, researchers are even now seeking to answer the question of whether deer become alarmed at the sight of hunters wearing bright orange camouflage suits or are merely amused.

Most of my own research into vision has been directed at determining how hunters and anglers see, and what can be done about it. The people I hunt and fish with all seem to have eyes the equivalent of twelve-power binoculars. Nothing is more annoying than having your friends constantly pointing out game at amazing distances. I am now on the brink of solving this problem once and for all.

Last weekend I was dove hunting with my friends Walt and Skip. Every so often they would squint off down the Snake River Canyon and shout at me, "Comin' up!" I would wheel around, gun at the ready, and there would be nothing there. After a few seconds, a speck would appear in the distance, eventually expanding into a dove, which I would scare the dickens out of as it whistled past. Then Skip would yell, "Comin' down!" and once again there would be nothing there. Well, that sort of thing can get on a person's nerves.

I decided to execute Ploy No. 18. "Comin' up!" I shouted. Skip and Walt both turned to face downcanyon. I walked over and got my lunch out of the pickup, opened a can of soda, and settled myself comfortably on the tailgate. After a while, Walt and Skip walked over and got out their lunches too. We were sitting there exchanging a few stories when a dove went past. Walt and Skip stared at it. "Boy," I said, "that ole dove was sure a far piece off down the canyon. I don't blame you fellas for not waiting for it."

One must be fairly immune to dirty looks if he is to get full enjoyment out of the use of Ploy No. 18.

One fellow I hunt with takes malicious pleasure in pointing to a white speck on a mountain off in the hazy distance and saying, "Goat."

My practice used to be to grab my binoculars and focus them on the white speck. Then I'd say, "Just a patch of snow! Ha! And you thought it was a goat, Fred!"

"It *is* a goat," Fred would reply. "See, it's moving along that ridge."

I'd look again through my binoculars, and sure enough, the white speck would be moving along the ridge.

"Well," I'd respond, "sometimes patches of snow move along ridges just like that this time of year."

Since a hunter can stand only so much humiliation, I started using Ploy No. 5 on Fred. Whenever he pointed at a distant white speck and said, "Goat," I'd reply, "Yes, I've been watching it for some time. A small billy, if I'm not mistaken. What do you think, Fred?"

Ploy No. 5 works wonderfully well. Nowadays a mountain goat could be standing on the hood of our car nibbling the windshield wipers and Fred wouldn't point to it and say, "Goat." And that's the way I like it.

Here's another technique I've used for keeping my eagle-eyed friends properly humble. I'll study a hillside for a few moments—any hillside will do as long as it's several hundred yards off—and then say casually, "Three deer up there. Two does and a fawn, if I'm not mistaken."

My friends stare at the hillside so hard beads of sweat form on their eyeballs. Finally, embarrassed, they start sweeping the hillside with binoculars.

"There's no deer up there," one of them growls.

"The tracks," I say. "Don't you see those three sets of tracks?"

"*Tracks?*"

"Yeah," I say. "But I see now they're at least a day old."

Occasionally someone will actually spot a deer on a hillside where I've indicated I've just seen one. One must remember to remain cool and detached in such cases and avoid blurting out things like "Really?" or "You're kidding me, right?" Such responses are almost always a dead giveaway.

Last spring a fishing buddy of mine looked down into the murky, swirling water by our boat and smugly reported, "I see the chironomids are hatching." I was impressed. A chironomid would have had to be the size of a volleyball for anybody to have seen it in that water.

"*Very good,* Bill!" I said.

Smiling with satisfaction, Bill took out a cigar and lit it. "Yep," he said presently, "the chironomids are hatching. I saw a piece of chironomid shell float past."

I realized immediately that with any more encouragement, the man could become a keen-observation fanatic.

"A piece of chironomid shell, hunh?" I said. "That's
a good sign. I've been seeing chironomid spoor in the
water, but it appeared to be several days old." Bill hasn't
mentioned a keen observation since.

Then there is the problem of dealing with illusions.
Obviously, the first thing any hunter must learn is not
to shoot at his illusions, those peculiar practical jokes
the eye is so fond of playing on us.

In early-morning darkness, I once kept an entire
party of hunters crouched breathless and freezing in the
snow while I watched a herd of dead trees cross over a
ridge and head in our direction. First light seeping
through the crack of dawn slowly revealed that I had
been watching not deer but frost-covered snags. Embarrassed, I turned to my companions, now also frost-
covered, and signaled for them to sneak around to the
far side of the mountain, just in case the dead trees
should catch our scent and make a break for it.

Distance often plays a part in the creation of illusions.
I have often observed the phenomenon in which hunters
who make a shot of 150 feet later judge the distance to
be not less than 300 yards. Strangely, hunters who make
a shot of 300 yards almost never think the distance was
only 150 feet. Further research may someday solve the
riddle of this strange phenomenon.

I once so misjudged the distance across a lake that it
nearly cost me my life. A resort owner had rented me
a little twelve-foot boat and a five-horse motor, assuring
me they were more than seaworthy enough to get me
across the lake. Even though the boat and motor ap-

peared to have been left behind by the Lewis and Clark expedition, it seemed to me he was probably right, since the lake didn't look that large. After all, I could see lichen growing on the far shore. Now I'm not sure whether the motor conked out just before or just after the storm hit, but it was about the time I discovered the lichen on the far shore was full-grown trees. It was a *big* lake! I was soon simultaneously performing CPR on the motor and contemplating how best to implant a five-horse outboard in a resort owner. The only question was whether to remove it from the boat first.

One of my scariest illusions occurred on a camping trip when I was a kid. Kenny Thompson, Vern Schulze, and I had returned to our camp late in the evening to discover a huge, batlike creature fluttering about the camp. The monster was about the size of our tent, and after throwing rocks at it for several minutes, we discovered that it *was* our tent. We were all immensely relieved, and later agreed it would be best if we didn't mention to anyone that we had tried to drive our tent out of camp by throwing rocks at it.

Several times while fishing a river in grizzly country I have had large tree stumps rear up in front of me and play havoc with my bodily functions. On the same river, a large gray rock with a bush growing out of it chased a friend of mine across the river and up a tree. He said later he purposely selected a young tree, because large rocks have trouble climbing the slender trunk.

Then there was the time I crawled on my belly all the way across a cow pasture to get a closeup wildlife photograph of a rusty 1938 Plymouth feeding in a creek. I did not make the precise identification of the species myself but was provided it by the farmer who owned the pasture. As he put it, "I thought—*heeeYAAAhooo!*—that dang ole '38 Plymouth—*WAAAAHHHee hee heee!*—was gonna spook before—*haahaaa! sniff! choke!*—you got to it!"

Actually, a rusty 1938 Plymouth coupe looks a lot more like a cow moose than you might suspect.

A Brief History
of Boats and Marriage

Young Harold Perkins and I were out in my workshop the other day discussing one of our favorite topics. Harold got married a while back, but as he says, he still likes "to look." Well just as Harold was saying, "Pat, this Megan has the sweetest little curves you ever saw," my wife, Bun, walked in. Ol' Bun just flipped out.

"Terrific!" Bun snapped. "That's really terrific, Harold! Here you are, married less than three months, with a baby on the way, and you're already carrying on like that. Boy, that is so disgusting! I would expect that sort of thing from old Whatsis here, but not from you, Harold."

I studied Harold, to see if he had developed any of the essential marital reflexes yet. I wasn't surprised to see that he hadn't. He stood there looking embarrassed and apologetic. I let him suffer for a few seconds, and then stepped in and saved him.

"What are you getting so upset about?" I said to Bun. "We're just talking about women."

"Women?" Bun said. "Oh. Gee, please excuse me, Harold. I thought you were talking about boats."

"Naw," I said. "Just beautiful women, the ones who find me so attractive."

"Yeah, I know the type," Bun said. "The ones who like pudgy old guys."

Before I could whittle a retort to a sharp point, she slipped away, chuckling fiendishly. I find fiendish chuckling very unbecoming in a woman, and I plan to tell Bun so, too.

"So where were we?" I said to Harold, who still seemed a bit shaken up. "Oh, you were telling me about Megan."

"Yeah, right," Harold said. "This Megan is a real beauty. She's a twenty-footer, tied up to the pier at Doc's Boat Works, if you want to take a look at her. But tell me something. How come Bun got so upset when she thought we were talking about boats?"

I was surprised that Harold knew so little about the facts of marital life. Here was a hip young man, twenty-four years old, married almost three months, baby on the way, and no one apparently had ever sat him down and had a man-to-man talk with him about boats and marriage. As I've often advocated, we need a boat-education course in the schools. Otherwise, youngsters are simply going to pick up on the streets and playgrounds a lot of misinformation about boats. Then they enter into matrimony, holy or otherwise, with their heads crammed full of nonsense. No wonder 50 percent of all marriages now end in divorce.

"Sit down, Harold," I said. "Let me tell you something about the relationship between a man, his wife, and his boats. First of all, the proper understanding of boats is essential to marital bliss. Otherwise, the reference to boats would not be included in marriage vows, as in 'Do you promise to love, honor, and obey your husband and not speak ill of his boats.' "

"Gee, boats weren't referred to in our marriage vows," Harold said.

"They weren't?" I said. "Too late to do anything about that now. You've got to slip the guy performing the ceremony an extra ten bucks to get that phrase in. Well worth the dough, too, I can tell you that."

"But what good does it do? Bun speaks ill of your boats all the time."

"Yeah, but she doesn't honor and obey me either. You see what I mean?"

"No."

"Well, there you go. You young guys today can't seem to follow a simple line of reasoning. Anyway, as I was about to say, since almost the beginning of humankind, men have been driven by this vague but powerful urge to cross over bodies of water without getting wet." I went on to give Harold a brief history of boats and wives, which is as follows.

In the beginning, or maybe a little before, early man tried to satisfy his urge for crossing bodies of water by running really fast over the surface of lakes, but that, as you know, proved unsuccessful, particularly for trolling. That also is one of the main reasons scientists now believe early man may have had webs between his toes, and probably between his ears, too.

Then, according to pictographs found on the walls of caves in Montana, which at that time was a small suburb of Kansas City, a man by the name of Org, or possibly Gor, discovered that by clinging to a log and kicking with his feet, he could propel himself across water. He started with a little twelve-foot log, moved up to a sixteen, then an eighteen, and finally a twenty-two-footer, a pattern followed even today by boat-buyers. Org told his mate, Gord, that he thought he really needed a thirty-footer, but she said, "Ye gods, Org, not another log! You already have four!" Oddly enough, this attitude of wives toward boats is still prevalent.

Org found the log not totally satisfactory as a flotation device. Seldom was he able to bring one of his logs up to planing speed, and then only because he was hotly pursued by a herd of venomous water spiders the size of sage grouse. Besides their other drawbacks, Org also found the logs difficult to trailer, not realizing the wheel hadn't yet been invented. For a while, he tried using Gord as a boat trailer but had too much trouble hooking up her lights, at the time merely small dabs of flaming pitch. Even now, wives cringe at the mention of boat-trailer lights. That is because one of the major marital functions of a wife is to stand behind the boat trailer and respond to her husband's questions, as he lies amid a tangle of wires beneath the towing vehicle: "Now what light is on? Are you sure it's the left turn signal? Cripes! Okay, now did the right taillight flicker? It didn't? Cripes!"

It finally occurred to Org that if the log were hollowed out, he could sit inside it and remain dry while crossing over water. He employed a clan of Neanderthals to hollow out a log with stone axes. Unfortunately, he made the mistake of paying them by the hour and soon went bankrupt. (Note: Some boat-repair shops appear to employ Neanderthals with stone axes even today; however, they are only crude replicas. True Neanderthal man became extinct thousands of years ago, much to his surprise and disappointment, because he had been looking forward to "Monday Night Football.") Three centuries later, the log was finally hollowed out, but, tragically, Org was not around to see his idea come to fruition. As a result, no one knew the reason for hollowing out the log in the first place, so it was used as a fruit bowl.

Then a young *Homo sapiens* by the name of Dick thought it might be fun to put the hollowed-out log in the river and paddle about in it, which he did. The significance of Dick's discovery, however, went unnoticed by the clan elders, who became concerned about the sanitary effects of a naked man paddling about in their fruit bowl. As one of the elders said, "You crazy, Dick! We got to eat out of that thing!" Thus are many of the great scientific advances misunderstood by ignorant and shortsighted leaders.

Eventually, the hollowed-out log became accepted as a means of getting about on water. Propulsion was accomplished by pushing or paddling the log about with sticks, but then a man by the name of Norman came up with an ingenious idea. He strapped his next-door neighbor, Ralph, to the stern of the boat and tossed a couple of the venomous water spiders in behind him. To Norman's delight, he discovered that he could by this means get two or three knots out of Ralph on a calm day. By adding or reducing the number of water spiders, he could control the speed of his boat. Little did Norman realize that he had invented not only the first outboard motor but also a crude form of the throttle. Fueled by nothing more than a few inexpensive water spiders, Ralph would roar about the lake for half an hour or more, often becoming quite hoarse.

When Norman told his wife, Vera, about his amazing invention, she could scarcely contain herself, finally shouting out, "I wish you would stop messing with that stupid hollow log and do some work around this place."

Even now, variations of this same cryptic plea reverberate through the homes of boaters, but so far remain indecipherable.

Sadly, Norman never lived to profit from his invention. He vanished one day after running out of spiders and asking Ralph to help him round up a few dozen to get back home on. Ralph came home alone, paddling the boat with the thighbone of a thesaurus. Everyone expected Norman eventually to return with wonderful tales about his adventures, although Ralph was fairly pessimistic about that possibility.

Ralph, incidentally, made his own contribution to science. He demonstrated how the thighbone of a thesaurus could be used for knocking some sense into people's heads. As a result Neanderthal man soon became extinct. Neanderthal woman, on the other hand, at last liberated from the drudgery of cavekeeping, went on to prosper and today puts in frequent appearances on "The Phil Donahue Show."

"Well," I told Harold, "that's all the time I have for the history of boats and wives. I think I'll go down to the pier and take a look at this Megan."

"You're going to absolutely love Meagan," Harold said.

At that moment Bun returned. "What about loving Megan?" she asked, her eyes narrowing to mean slits.

"Uh, she's the new barmaid down at Kelly's Bar and Grill," Harold said.

The kid learns fast, I'll say that for him.

Boating Disorders

For several years I was a student of Sigmund Freud. Then someone told me Freud was dead, which explained why his classes were so boring. Why am I always last to be told? If you ask me, they are carrying the concept of faculty tenure much too far.

After graduating from the university, I set up shop as a psychiatrist. Business flourished, despite my degrees either in agronomy or English literature. The State Licensing Board for Psychiatrists from time to time questioned my qualifications, particularly my inability to spell *psychiatry* the same way twice. I promised to work on my spelling and refer wealthy patients to the board members. They said, "In that case, don't worry about the spelling. It's your positive attitude that counts."

My specialty was boating disorders. Many people buy a boat without the slightest notion that it will soon dominate their lives. They see a boat in a showroom and it looks so innocent and seaworthy sitting there on a shag carpet. They take the new boat home, park it in the driveway, and start to go in the house. The boat says, "Hey, what do you think you're doing? You can't leave me out here in the driveway. Get that stupid car out of the garage and put me in there, until you can build me a suitable shelter of my own."

"Gee, I didn't know boats talked," the new owner says.

"I didn't know boats talked!" the boat mimics. "You haven't heard anything yet, buster. I want my oil-injection system checked by a specialist, new rollers on this cheap trailer you bought, a decent depth finder installed, a . . . what's that, a dog? Get rid of the dog. You're not going to have time for a dog. From now on, it's just you and me, pal, so hop to it."

Most of my patients come to me complaining of the demands their boats place on them. "I hate to mention this, Doc, but I even hear my boat ordering me around."

"Hmmmmm," I say. "Well, as long as you do what your boat orders, you'll probably be perfectly safe. I do everything my boat tells me and it hasn't seriously harmed me yet. Any other problems?"

Because I myself am owned by several boats, I have an excellent understanding of my patients' boating disorders, mostly *nautical dementia.* Just last week some idiot drifted his crummy little scow of a boat into my brand-new Helga IV and put this hideous scratch on her hull. I've had to sit up with her every night since, listening to her cries of "I'm not new anymore, I'm not new anymore!" It tears my heart out.

But enough of my own traumas. Here are some of my more interesting cases as a boating psychiatrist.

Case #47   Milo S. came to me complaining of a lack of identity. I explained to him that the problem was rooted in the fact that he used only the initial S for a last name. After going through his billfold and not finding any iden- tification, I read off to him a series of last names begin- ning with S until he found one he liked—Smith. I agreed to take him on as a patient if he would pay my fee in cash rather than by check. He reluctantly accepted those terms, and then babbled out the following tale of woe.

Milo had been a take-charge kind of guy all his life. He was tall, handsome, smart, prosperous, and a born leader. One day he bought a large, expensive boat and trailered it out to a launch area. A half-dozen or so fishermen were there fiddling with their crummy little boats when Milo arrived with his magnificent, gleaming craft and a brace of highly attractive female companions, which often come as accessories with such boats. The fishermen stared in awe and envy at the expensive boat, even as they ogled the attractive female companions.

Milo backed his boat trailer straight as an arrow down the launch ramp. The boat slid gracefully into the waves, as one of the attractive female companions held fast to the bow line. Milo stepped from the cab of his powerful pickup truck, expertly checked to see that everything was shipshape. Satisfied, he climbed confidently back into his pickup and roared back toward the parking area— *dragging his new boat up the concrete ramp after him!* He had forgotten to unsnap the winch line from the bow!

When Milo stepped from the cab of the pickup to see what all the racket was about and beheld his new two- ton boat sitting high and dry on the corrugated concrete, his hair began to thin and whiten. His deep-bronze tan faded into a pinkish pallor. He lost six inches in height, and his muscles turned to flab. Immediately, a line of three hundred boaters trailering boats formed at the blocked ramp and began honking their horns. Milo felt

like an insufferable boob. "You insufferable boob!"
screamed one of his attractive female companions,
thereby confirming Milo's own self-image. He then
slunk off to the nearest telephone booth, called his mom,
and asked if he could have his old room back and had
she by any chance saved his teddy.

Thus can boating turn strong men into spineless
wimps in the blink of an eye. Milo is now participating
in a group session I hold on Wednesday nights for insufferable boobs. There's not much chance he will be
cured, if for no other reason than that I was 147th in
line at the ramp he blocked.

Case #89   Curtis M. came to me suffering from a boating disorder that left him incapable of saying anything
except "I forgot to put the plug in! I forgot to put the
plug in!" I gave him a shock treatment, in which my
secretary sprang stark naked out of a closet and hit him
in the face with a cream pie. "That will be all, Miss
Evans," I said. "I see the patient has recovered the power
of coherent speech." And indeed he had. Curtis went
on to relate the following bizarre tale.

He had just started a new job and thought he might
make a few points with the boss by taking him and his
wife out for a boat ride. Neither the boss nor the wife,
whom we'll call Mr. and Mrs. Jones for the purpose of
avoiding nuisance litigation, had had any experience
with boating. Prior to the outing, Curtis had turned a
garden hose on the interior of his fishing boat and
blasted out several years' accumulation of fish scales,
dried worms, rotten salmon eggs, rusty fishing lures,
half-eaten sandwiches, and the usual sand and mud, all
of which, as experienced fishermen know, are applied

to the inside of fishing boats for the purpose of sound-proofing. Curtis, of course, realized that it would take at least two years to get the boat back in shape for serious fishing, but he thought the inconvenience was worth it to impress his boss.

Curtis launched the boat, boarded his guests, and roared out across the lake at a nifty clip. He talked a little boat talk to Mr. and Mrs. Jones—"bow, stern, lines, blaw blaw, pitch, beam, starboard, port, blaw blaw"—because boat talk increases passengers' confidence in the skill of the skipper and puts them at ease. After a bit, Mr. and Mrs. Jones began asking boating questions.

"My goodness, what are all those switches for?" Mrs. Jones asked.

Curtis was very proud of all his switches. For many years, he had been too poor to own a boat with a single switch. He happily explained that the switches were for running lights, live well, bilge pump (broken), exhaust fans, and the like.

"Well, what have we here?" asked Mr. Jones. "This is a complicated-looking instrument."

"That's my electronic fish-finder, sir," Curtis explained. "It indicates how deep the fish are."

"And what's this little thing?" asked Mrs. Jones.

"Oh, that's a plug," said Curtis. "It fits in a drain hole in the stern of the boat. If the drain plug isn't in, the lake drains into the boat. Ha ha."

"Ha ha," said Mrs. Jones. "So this is a spare plug then?"

"And over here," said Curtis, "are what we call personal flotation devices, commonly referred to as life jackets. Why don't you each try one of them on, while I turn the boat around and head for shore?"

With water lapping against his ankles, Curtis made

some calculations: "If X gallons of water gush into a boat every minute and Y minutes have passed and the boat travels at the rate of Z miles per hour . . ." Never being good at story problems, Curtis was still working on his calculations when the boat sank to its gunnels. "Now here's something you'll find interesting," Curtis said to his guests. "This boat floats even full of water and with three people in it. In fact, you could take a chain saw and cut the boat into three equal pieces and it would still float with three people." His boss replied that as soon as he could find a chain saw, he was going to cut Curtis into three equal pieces.

As I explained to Curtis, almost every boater at one time or another forgets to put in the plug. That is why the psychiatry business flourishes. One of my patients launched his boat from the trailer, tied it up to the dock, and left to drive his truck and trailer up to the parking area. When he returned, all he could see of his boat was the bow line straining at a sharp angle down into the water. On all such occasions, even though you haven't seen another person in the last three weeks, a crowd instantly assembles and shouts gleefully, "You forgot to put the plug in!"

As my contribution to the mental and emotional well-being of my fellow boaters and patients, I have rede-signed the boat plug so that the instant you put the boat in water, you are alerted to the fact that the plug is missing. Traditionally, of course, you learned of a truant plug only when you were out in the middle of the lake and noticed water lapping against your ankles. The reason for this is that the standard plug is only an inch or two in diameter, allowing the water to spurt in unnoticed until you are far from shore. The plug I've designed, on the other hand, is only slightly smaller than a manhole cover. You put the boat in the water, and—presto!—it sinks. It slides off the trailer and goes instantly to the bottom, before lives can be endangered. The Coast Guard may require my plug on all new boats as a safety device.

I also gave Curtis a method for dealing with the embarrassment associated with forgotten boat plugs. You should always carry a clipboard, a few sheets of paper, and a pencil in the boat with you. As you are piloting your foundering boat back to shore, you wait until you are within a few yards of the assembling crowd of onlookers, people whose only purpose in life is to show up on the scene of forgotten plugs and shout, "Bet you forgot your plug! Hahahahah!" You then pull out your clipboard and start making marks on the paper with the pencil, exclaiming, "Wow! Floated twelve point seven minutes with the plug out! The engineers won't believe the results of the test!" This little ploy works very well, unless you have other occupants aboard, in which case they should be discouraged from leaping out of the boat, kissing the ground, and yelling, "Cripes! We made it! I thought we were all going to drown!"

Case #137 On his first visit to my office, Delbert J. displayed symptoms of paranoia, glancing over his shoulder, peering under my desk and table, and even looking in the closet. He shut the closet door and said, "Do you know you have a naked lady standing in your closet with a cream pie?"

"Yes," I said. "We have a shock treatment to perform this afternoon, but it has nothing to do with you. What seems to be your problem, Delbert?"

"People keep standing on my face," he said.

"I see," I said, realizing the poor chap was suffering from delusions, although that did not entirely explain my urge to stand on his face. "Why don't you tell me about it?"

Delbert and his wife had been fishing at a remote lake and were returning home late at night along a deserted highway. Delbert had heard that the Mean Nasties motorcycle gang often used the highway. He could not shake a premonition of impending doom. Suddenly, he heard *whoppity whoppity whoppity* on the road behind him and realized his boat trailer had blown a tire. His spare tire for the trailer turned out to be flat, too, which was strange, because he had checked it just nine years before and it was okay then.

His wife volunteered to stand guard over the boat and trailer while Delbert drove off in search of an open service station, which probably didn't even exist. Delbert said he wouldn't hear of her volunteering for such a risky chore. He suggested cutting cards. Delbert lost. Toward dawn, the Mean Nasties came by, returning from a combined picnic and firebombing. Delbert helped them strip his boat, after which they showed their appreciation by not killing him, although they did take turns standing on his face. Eighteen hours later, his wife returned with the inflated spare and a new hairdo.

The following week, Delbert was out on another lake. His boat was nearly out of gas, a storm was blowing in, and it was almost dark. Delbert decided he had better head back to the launch area. He was cruising along when he saw an emergency flare fired from a big sleek speedboat. He went over to offer assistance to the boaters and discovered they were the Mean Nasties. They recognized him.

"Hey, man, we're sorry we stripped your boat and

stood on your face," one of them said. "It was all in fun. Now how about giving us a tow back to the launch ramp? Our motor conked out and it will take us two hours to paddle back. Two hours!"

Delbert told the Mean Nasties off, gestured crudely at them, and roared off, laughing. When he neared the launch ramp, he discovered boats lined up practically to the middle of the lake.

"What's wrong?" he asked a fisherman.

"Some insufferable boob forgot to unsnap his winch line and dragged his boat up high and dry on the ramp. The ramp is blocked!"

"How long before they get it unblocked?" Delbert asked.

"Three hours."

Scarcely was Delbert out of the hospital than he found himself in another predicament. He had just launched his boat and was attempting to start the motor when he noticed he was drifting toward a brand-spanking-new craft. The proud owner of the craft was out spit-polishing the chrome fittings. As Delbert frantically tried to start his motor, his boat drifted closer and closer to the new boat, the owner of which was now jumping up and down and trying to wave him off. Then, horribly, as Delbert jerked helplessly at the pull cord on his motor, the two boats grated together in one long hideous *Scraaaaaaatttttttttcccchhhh!* The new boat was permanently scarred, the owner sick with grief. Before he could get his face stood on, Delbert cranked up his motor and sped off.

"What do you think, Doc?" he asked me. "Can I be cured?"

I now remembered why I recognized Delbert. "Maybe," I said. "We will try a new technique. Please lie down flat on the floor. Face up."

Try Not to Annoy Me

I never met an outdoorsman I didn't like, although I find a good many of them annoying. Being a methodical person, I have entered into my computer all the outdoorsmen I know and categorized them according to annoyance. A few of the several hundred categories are as follows.

Methodical Person Boy, this guy really gets on my nerves. You're already late getting started on a camping trip, and he will say, "All right, now let's make sure we have everything." He pulls out a checklist four feet long and begins checking off items: "Toothpaste, okay, toothbrush, okay, mouthwash, okay, toothpicks—where are the toothpicks? Anybody seen the toothpicks? Okay. Dental floss . . ." The guy will spend ten minutes checking off items related just to oral hygiene, never mind that once he is in hunting camp he brushes his teeth with a finger dipped in whiskey and then only on Wednesdays. His breath kills trees. His is the acid rain of bad breath. I once saw a dressed-out elk get up and run three hundred yards just because this guy breathed on it. But he insists on being methodical. Finally, we, his hunting companions, throw his junk in the truck and him and his list in on top of it. "Toilet tissue!" he cries. "I didn't check off toilet tissue!" Someone then makes a crude remark about his list.

Easily Annoyed Person Some little thing will go wrong on a hunting trip, such as forgetting to bring any toilet tissue, and the guy will say, "Really, I find this very annoying." Or he will say, "All right, who's got mud on his boots? Who's tracking mud into the tent? Boy, is this annoying!" While he is thinking up new annoyances, he forgets to set the handbrake on the hunting vehicle, which runs over our tent and leaks crankcase oil all over our grub, and he says, "Complain, complain! All you guys do is complain. It's really, you know, annoying." I find persons who get annoyed easily particularly annoying.

Graduate of the Will Rogers School of Philosophy Three days in a hunting camp with this fellow and you're ready for the intensive-care unit of a psychiatric hospital. In real life, he wears a three-piece suit and speaks like John Houseman "making money the old-fashioned way." In hunting camp, he wears a sloppy old Stetson and turns into Will Rogers, the cowboy philosopher. "I never met a man I didn't like, but you birds are shore puttin' me to the test," he will say. Almost nothing occurs that he can't direct his cowboy philosophy at:

"If we could somehow feed some of this coffee to the politicians we'd git that mess in Washington cleaned up real fast."

"What they need in Washington, D.C., is a class in gun safety. Hardly a day goes by there that some politician don't shoot off his mouth."

"If you ask me, the national debt is like this here elk steak. The more the politicians chew on it, the larger it gits."

And so on and on and on. Hunting with a cowboy philosopher is like . . . is like . . . Well, I can't think of anything it's like, but it's real hard on the nerves. I guess cowboy philosophy is something you have to be born with.

Explainers I am easily annoyed by people who feel they must explain everything to you. "The reason you can't get that fire started is the wood's too wet." Oh? That never would have occurred to me. "You know why that fish snapped your leader? Your leader was too light." Gee, I would never have guessed. "The reason a compass always points north is . . ." Half their sentences begin, "The way that works is . . ." Explainers apparently assume you have spent your entire life inside a paper bag and therefore have not the slightest notion of the reason for anything. But wait until you actually do need something explained, such as why your vehicle suddenly expires forty miles back in the wilderness, or better yet, how to get the thing started again. "Beats me," they say. "You expect me to know everything?"

Fixers You notice a loose screw on your fishing reel and start to tighten it. "Here, let me do that," says the fixer, prying the screwdriver out of your hand. Or you start to adjust the idle on your outboard motor. "Here, let me do that," the fixer says, shoving you out of the way. Fixers are of the belief that you are totally incompetent to perform the simplest task. If you're buttoning your hunting jacket, they say, "Here, let me do that for you." Fixers are basically good-hearted chaps and really don't annoy me that much. I've noticed that when it comes to wading into icy water up to my armpits to adjust a one-ton boat evenly on a trailer in the dark, a fixer will always step forward and say, "Here, let me hold your coat for you."

Impressionists You are up to your armpits in icy water trying to adjust a one-ton boat on a trailer in the dark, and the impressionist yells, "Hey, Pat, look! Here's my impression of George Burns talking to Groucho Marx." I was once on a fishing trip with an impressionist who got stuck in a John Wayne impression and couldn't get out of it. "Pass me the salt, Pilgrim," he'd say, "and don't be all day about it neither." I finally had to shoot him.

Stand-Up Comics These guys tell jokes end to end, always beginning, "Did you hear the one about . . . ?"
    "Yeah, we heard it," you say.
    "But probably not this version of it. Henry Kissinger, Richard Nixon, and a hippie are on this plane to-gether . . ." There is no way to stop stand-up comics. After the fourth joke in a row, shoot them.

Take-Charge Guys Every outing of more than one person has a take-charge guy: "Okay, the way we're going to do this is, Pat, you do this, Fred, you do that, and Arnie, you do the other thing. Everybody knows what he's supposed to do? Good. We'll meet back here at four o'clock." The take-charge guy is a born leader. Unfortunately, as we all know, born leaders often have the IQ of a rock. That's what makes them so easy to follow.

Whiners   Your vehicle suddenly expires forty miles back in the wilderness, and the whiner says, "I knew something like this would happen! Now what are we going to do? Why do these things always happen to me when I'm out with you guys? I just wish you would check these things out to make sure they're running properly before you haul me all the way out here in the middle of nowhere on a wild-goose chase."

The only fit punishment for a whiner is to lock him up inside the vehicle with the Explainer, the Cowboy Philosopher, and the Impressionist. Sure, it's cruel and unusual punishment, but it serves the wimp right.